D1597052

Winston-Salem

Friedland, southwest of Salem, was settled in the
early 1770s by Moravians who came to
Wachovia from Broadbay, Maine, having become
dissatisfied with their location there.
They were shipwrecked off the cost of Virginia en
route, arriving in Salem in 1769. They
established a separate church there in the late
1770s and in 1847 put up the above building,
the second Friedland Church, which was used until 1952.

Courtesy of Bill East

The auction sale of tobacco having proved successful, in 1873 a stock company erected this warehouse on Fourth Street at the corner of Trade. It was leased, in 1876, by M. W. Norfleet, and the name changed to Piedmont, being Winston's third such establishment. At the time of this photograph, the building was being offered for sale at auction, and would soon be torn down for the erection of the Masonic Temple. The site is now occupied by the Rite Aide drug store, on the mall.

Courtesy of the Frank Jones Collection

Winston-Salem

A Pictorial History by Fambrough L. Brownlee

Design by Edward A. Conner
Donning Company/Publishers
Norfolk, Virginia

Copyright ©1977 by Fambrough L. Brownlee

All rights reserved, including the right to reproduce this book in any form whatsoever without permission in writing from the publisher, except for brief passages in connection with a review. For information, write The Donning Company/Publishers, 253 West Bute Street, Norfolk, Virginia 23510.

Library of Congress Cataloging in Publication Data:

Brownlee, Fambrough L.   1943-
Winston-Salem: a pictorial history.

1. Winston-Salem, N.C.—History—Pictorial works.
2. Winston-Salem, N.C.—Description—Views.   1. Title.
F264.W8B76   975.6'67   77-2177
ISBN 0-915442-26-4

Printed in the United States of America

The first Winston Municipal Building, designed by Glen Brown and W. E. Hall, was erected by Miller Brothers in 1892 at a cost of forty-five thousand dollars. The building stood at the corner of Fourth and Main and housed the city administrative offices with the jail located upstairs. At the rear were the armory and the meat market. At the left is F. C. Brown's dry goods store, number one West Fourth, and next to it the hardware store of Brown, Rogers and Company, while on the right, on Main Street, are the clothing stores of Robbins Brothers and C. Summerfield and Company. At least four people died on this corner during the race riot of 1918. In 1927 the Municipal Building was torn down to make way for the R. J. Reynolds office building. The clocks were removed to the tower of Calvary Moravian Church, where they remain today.

Courtesy of Bill East

For my wife, Mary
and my son, Mont,
whose patience made
it possible.

Contents

Pleasant Henderson Hanes (left) poses for this 1918 photograph with his grandchildren and workers at his "Burke Farm," near the present site of Forsyth Memorial Hospital. The children are, left to right in the foreground: Rosalie Hanes (Rice), Nona Hanes (Porter), Clair Hanes (Follin), and Spencer Hanes, Jr. Behind Nona Hanes is Lizora Schoolfield (Miller). The man in the vest behind Spencer Hanes is George Feezor, general manager of all Hanes farms. At his right, with the cap, is his son, George Feezor, Jr.

Courtesy of Mrs. Clair Hanes Follin

Introduction

Each winter when the air had just the right "bite" to it, Pleasant Henderson Hanes had his grandchildren fetched from school to his Burke Farm on the old road to Clemmons. The purpose of the holiday from school was not pleasure; they were to witness the time-honored ritual of hog killing. And like most of the other things Mr. Hanes did, this exhibition had a calculated reason behind it. He explained to the children: "I don't want you ever to forget where you came from." Pleasant Henderson Hanes knew what he was talking about. He was born on a farm in Davie County, not far from where my grandfather was reared. At a tender age, he went to work for Brown Brothers as a "drummer," selling tobacco on the road from town to town. He was known as one of the best, a man who got up early to beat his competitors to the punch. That early experience in hard work on the farm and on the road would serve him well in the building of two empires, in tobacco and textiles. He never forgot, and he wanted his grandchildren to know what it took to make good.

Mr. Hanes' philosophy blends nicely with the reason for the making of this book. It is not intended to serve as a comprehensive history of Winston-Salem. It is, rather, an attempt to show, in pictures and as little text as possible, what it took for two towns of vastly dissimilar nature, growing up side by side, to make good. The Twin City of today, with its fine factories, banks, schools, and cultural organizations, did not spring up overnight in the Muddy Creek watershed. It was, rather, put together slowly, and with great effort on the part of many people, over a period that now spans 225 years. Carl Sandburg, who lived for many years in the mountains of western North Carolina, once wrote: "When men forget what they have done and where they came from, they have lost the foundation for going forward." I hope that this book will provide the beginning of that foundation for many of its readers.

Fambrough L. Brownlee

Tom Hege, below, and his grandnephew, Frank Jones, combined to give Winston-Salem a legacy of pictorial documentation that spans eighty years. Hege, one of Winston's first Seventh Day Adventists, was a genuine character of his times, advertising himself as an "Art Glass Blower, Photographer and Experimenter in General." He had a portable organ, and it is said that he would set up on the courthouse square on Saturday afternoons and play until a crowd had gathered, then commence a little "sidewalk evangelism." But it is through his camera work that we best know him and the towns of Winston and Salem in the 1890s.

He and Frank Jones shared, along with a penchant for strange manners of spelling, an interest in photography. Frank Jones was a photographer for the Winston-Salem *Journal and Sentinel* for nearly forty years. His interest in history, present at an early age as evidenced by his notebooks from the 1930s, led him to collect old photographs, while busily recording with his own camera the events of his day. Historians and the citizens of Winston-Salem owe a great debt to the granduncle and the grandnephew.

Courtesy of the Frank Jones Collection

Nicholas Ludvig, Count Zinzendorf of Saxony, took in the resurgent membership of the Unitas Fratrum in June 1722, sheltering them on one of his estates from the attempted persecution of the Catholic Church and other Protestant sects. A man of education and breeding, his odd ideas alternately improved and threatened to destroy the growing community of Brethren. He was instrumental in the expansion of Moravian missionary activity, but it was his objection to direct recruiting of members that prevented the Moravian Church from growing into a large denomination. In the summer of 1976, the last building in Winston-Salem to bear his name, the old Zinzendorf Laundry, was torn down as a part of the Old Salem restoration project.

Courtesy of Bill East

Bishop August Gottlieb Spangenberg selected the site for the Wachovia tract. In 1752, he rode on horseback the length of the North Carolina colony. He and the members of his party suffered such privations as insects, snow-storms and malaria. They got lost near Blowing Rock, at the headwaters of the Yadkin and New Rivers, before finally finding their way to the three forks of the muddy creek that would become the Moravians' new home in the Carolina colony. It was Spangenberg who suggested the name "Der Wachau," after one of Count Zinzendorf's estates, that in its Latin form would distinguish the Moravian lands from those of their neighbors.

Courtesy of Bill East

Prehistory 8000 B.C. - 1751 A.D.

The river now known as the Yadkin rises in the Blue Ridge Mountains between the town named for Daniel Boone and the windy place called Blowing Rock. It plunges down the escarpment southeastwardly for almost twenty miles before curling back to the northeast where it flows gently, steadily widening, through a valley of rich agricultural bottomland, flanked on the left by the Blue Ridge and on the right by the Brushy Mountains. The river travels nearly sixty miles before beginning a gradual turning to the east, passing near another town bearing the Boone name, twenty miles more, then assumes an "S" configuration, throwing out first a bend to the east, and then a second bend to the west. Here the water is a rich brown color, and here it is joined by the waters of the muddy creek, to flow on down the piedmont plateau, becoming the Pee Dee, across the sandhills of South Carolina, becoming the Great Pee Dee, finally emptying into the Atlantic Ocean near Georgetown, South Carolina.

By at least 8000 B.C. people inhabited this river valley. Roaming the forest with their stone-pointed weapons they found a plentiful supply of game. The river teemed with fish, turtles, snakes, and mussels. The density of the population increased. At some point, the men began calling the river by name, the Atkin or Yatkin or Yeatkin. The meaning is a matter of contention: "Tall Trees," says one source, or "Peaceful Water." One local legend has it that when the first white settlers came to the eastern bank, the men of the forest stood on the other side and called, "Yeatkin! Yeatkin!", meaning "Come across and fight." Whatever the meaning, the quality of life along the river was good, and as new people drifted in from the Hudson River Valley and the Great Lakes, populations began to stabilize. By around 1400 A.D., a major village had begun to grow up on the east bend of the river. Little is known about the inhabitants. Archaeological evidence indicates that they built round lodges, the center of which became their burial sites at death. They made simple clay pots and pipes and had little apparent taste for ornamental devices. Certainly they hunted and fished for much of their food, with mussels forming a principal portion of their diet. Oddly, there is little evidence of agricultural activity. Normally, a large, stable population would drive away most of the game in a short time, forcing the adoption of agriculture to supplement the dwindling supply of meat. But here the usual bits of charred corn and other evidences of food growing are not present. It is, therefore, possible that the people who settled this

village became traders. Although located to the north and west of the main trading path in the piedmont region, the village boasted an effective signpost in the form of a neighboring mountain, featuring a bald granite knob that could be readily recognized for miles in any direction. Add to this a nearby shallow ford, created by a natural outcropping of rock, and the trading hypothesis gathers strength.

At any rate, the village flourished, and by the time Gregory the Patriarch had gathered his little band, "The Brethren of the Laws of Christ," together near Lititz in the 1450s, satellite villages had begun to spring up in the Yadkin flood-plain and along the banks of the three forks of the muddy creek. And by

On November 7, 1753, while still in Virginia, the little band of Moravian settlers who would found Bethabara saw "the Pilot Mountain in North Carolina, and rejoiced to think that we should soon see the boundary of Carolina, and set foot in our own dear land." The distinctive knob that had guided the Indians and the long-hunters would serve the Moravians as more than a landmark. Mention is made in the diaries of trips to the area for the procurement of granite, but one may surmise that the granite was no more important than the sheer joy of the view, such as this one from the little pinnacle looking past the knob at other mountains in the Sauratown range.

Photo by Fam Brownlee

9

the time that the "Admiral of the Ocean Sea" set sail in search of the fabled East Indies, land navigators were already using the pilot knob as a marker designating a village of nearly five hundred souls. Long before Walter Ralegh's men returned to the enigma of their missing Roanoke Island colony, the village on the river was past its peak. No real evidence records its demise. Migratory patterns, intertribal wars, a shortage of fish and game, disruption of trade or the coming of the first white "long-hunters" are only a few of the possible explanations for the disappearance of the village that stood in the shadow of the pilot knob. The people who lived there were, by all evidence, simple people, yet their village endured for at least two hundred years. If the settlement had a name, no one knows what it was. Many years later, a descendant of a man thought to have been a chieftain in the area named it, after his forebear, Donnoha.

In 1769, the half-timbered Single Brothers' House was completed. As the population expanded, the Brethren added a workshop behind the house in 1771, and in 1786 built a brick addition on the south side of the main house. Because of the increasing frequency of disturbances and breaking of rules, the choir was broken up in June 1823 and the space apportioned to various interests, including the boys' school. The Brothers' House is seen here around the turn of the twentieth century, after clapboard had been placed over the half-timbered walls. The building is now restored to its original appearance, part of it being open to visitors, while the remainder serves as offices of Old Salem, Incorporated.

Courtesy of the Frank Jones Collection

A Beginning in the Wilderness 1752-1772

It was not easy coming down the "Great Wagon Road." They recorded it in their journal. Trouble in Maryland with unruly Irishmen. Gravity-defying inclines. Rocks and ruts that dismembered equipment. The countless rivers and streams that had to be crossed at peril to life and property. And an occasional feeling of being lost, completely.

Faith carried them through it. On the worst of days they were able to find something good to report to their Lord at evening prayer. And upon arrival in their promised land, providence brought them a good omen in the form of an abandoned log house, shelter from torrential rains. Occasion for a love feast if ever there had been one.

They were not the first. The long-hunters had preceded them, and even they had found people on the land, the other men, craftsmen of the forest trail. Neither were they the pioneers. Already to the north and west of them the beginnings of plantations had been made.

In 1747-48 Morgan Bryan and others had settled along the Yadkin River. William Linville, who would later give his name to a mountain, a river, a town, and a spectacular waterfall, lived near the present Clemmons, on what would later be the Lasater estate. To the west of him, James Carter had taken up land that would become Joseph Williams' Panther Creek settlement. To the north, above the shallow ford, Samuel Davis had taken over what would later be part of George Brooks' plantation, and immediately across the river was George Forbush, whose name endures in the area to this day. By 1750 Squire Boone had brought his wife Sarah and his children, among them the explorer Daniel, into the area, and in early 1753, months before the first Moravian settlers arrived in Bethabara, Edward Hughes established a tavern at the shallow ford crossing.

But these members of the congregation of the United Brethren were unique in the North Carolina piedmont. First, they were a peaceful people, simple but literate, come to a hard-fisted land where formal learning was not listed among the cardinal virtues. Second, in a time when men took what land they could get in royal grants and built when and where they were able, the brethren had a plan, carefully devised by congregational elders, to build a town, actually two towns, a temporary "House of Passage," and, using that as a base, the permanent house of peace. And finally, in a countryside where no church, not even a brush arbor one, could be seen for at least a day's journey in any direction, they brought a stubborn, unwavering faith in their God. It was the unyielding quality of this third factor that would see them through the trials brought on by the first two.

They arrived at the first town site, Bethabara, on November 17, 1753, led by two ministers, Jacob Loesch and Bernard Adam Grube. That night they held the first love feast on the 98,985 acre Wachau tract and, after resting the next day, Sunday, began on Monday clearing land for their first planting.

They were hard workers, these Moravians, and through their incredible industriousness in less than two years they had built no less than twenty structures, including a Gemeinhaus (church and meeting house), a mill, pottery, tannery, and blacksmith shop, and a two-story house for the single brothers. In addition they had cut two roads through the forest, one to the river and one to the "Great Wagon Road" down which they had come, giving them a connection with the growing village of Salisbury to the south. Also in that second year, as unrest caused by the French and Indian War spilled over into the South, the brothers built a palisade around the greater part of their little town.

The relationship between the Moravians and the neighboring Indians was generally good. The Indians liked the easy handouts available at the "Dutch Fort" and tolerated the Moravian concern for the spiritual well-being of "those poor savages." But as the tempo of the raids in other parts of the state increased, the Brethren put aside, temporarily, their tradition of pacifism and formed a militia company to protect their settlement. When the raids began to reach into the Yadkin Valley, the little fort was overwhelmed by a surge of refugees, some from as far away as Virginia. Consequently, in the late spring of 1759, a site was selected in the nearby Black Walnut Bottom, and sixteen couples, half Moravians and half outsiders, moved out to found the new town of Bethania.

In 1760, the previously friendly Cherokees joined in the mayhem. Tales of close calls in the woods were rampant, and a number of people on outlying farms were killed. But the determination of the white settlers was strong, and the Cherokees fell back before the expanding population. By 1761 they were gone from most of the Yadkin Valley and the Moravians could return to their plans for a house of peace.

In 1764, Brother Frederick William Marshall, Oeconomus (chief executive) for Wachovia, submitted several possible sites for the new town to the "lot." Three tiny scrolls, one for "Yes," one for "No," and an indefinite blank, were placed in a wooden bowl and drawn to answer the carefully worded questions. For each site, the answer was "No." Again, on February 14, 1765, the question of a site was put to the lot. This time, the answer was "Yes." In May, Christian Gottlieb Reuter began surveying the 3,159 acre tract that lay, nearly in the center of Wachovia, along the south face of a long ridge, bounded by three creeks: the Wach (Salem), Lech (Brushy Fork) and Petersbach. The others began cutting a road through the forest from Bethabara to the new town site.

By January of 1766, the road was complete, and on the sixth of that month the felling of trees began in Salem. The Brethren took their daily text from Isaiah: "I will defend this city." On January 19, eight men moved into their newly completed log cabin, the first building erected in Salem.

Adam Spach, who founded the Friedburg Church in 1769, settled south of Salem near Abbott's Creek in 1754. Soon thereafter he built this house, known simply as the "Rock House." Thinking to use it as a fortress in case of Indian attack, he located it over a spring, with a basement large enough to shelter his livestock, and provided loopholes for firing. But during the Indian uprisings he, like most others in the area, sought shelter within the palisades at Bethabara.

Photo by Harry Peterson

The Reverend Frederic William Marshall, son of a German army officer and trained for a military career at the University of Leipzig, became, instead, a Moravian minister and the first leader of the Salem congregation. Appointed *Oeconomus,* or super-intendent, of temporal affairs in 1763, he became one of the most powerful men ever to live in Wachovia. By the time of his death on February 11, 1802, he had served in nearly every leadership capacity possible in the Moravian community. Among the Salem populace, only the surveyor, Christian Gottlieb Reuter, and Traugott Bagge even began to approach him in influence on the events of the early years of the House of Peace.

Courtesy of the Frank Jones Collection

Streets were laid out and the site for the main square selected. Two years later the square had to be moved a block south because the water system was incapable of supplying the upper end of the original site. Another cabin was put up, and in late spring work began on the first permanent house. In August, Joseph Mueller, a gunsmith, began making brick and tile, the first manufacturing operation in the new town. In October the first permanent house was finished and the foundation laying for the second begun.

Under the capable direction of Marshall, the work went forward, with time off only for an occasional love feast, commemorating such worthy events as a visit to the site by eight single sisters. Reuter, a virtual Renaissance man, was particularly helpful, supplying many of the sometimes esoteric skills required in the founding of a wilderness village.

On November 13, 1771, the Gemeinhaus was consecrated and the Salem congregation became a separate entity, with its own diary, written for ten years in English because Marshall desired it so. As Oeconomus and head of the Aeltesen Conferenz, which had charge of spiritual affairs in the community, Marshall was the most powerful man in the Wachovia settlement. Traugott Bagge headed the Aufseher Collegium, overseers of secular matters. In the spring of 1772 Marshall took on even more power when he became head of the Grosse Helfer Conferenz, made up of members of the Aeltesen and the Collegium, along with other assorted leaders of the village. The Conferenz was supposedly limited to advisory functions, but had, in fact, a powerful influence upon the lives of every person in the community. And that community had become the largest in Wachovia, with a population of 120. Bethania came second, with 105, while Bethabara, which had, as planned, fed most of its people into the new town, was down to 54. Salem had a school for boys, begun in December 1771, and a day school for little girls, begun in April 1772 by Sister Elizabeth Oesterlein. The gains made had not been free of cost. Because of their insular communist system and the prosperity it brought, the Salemites were both envied and suspected by their neighbors. The Moravians' conservative approach to every issue was particularly infuriating to those who were trying to bring about changes in the administration of taxes and the courts. When the Regulator movement reached the flashpoint, in 1771, the Moravians found themselves in what would soon become a familiar position. The

Regulators had, no doubt, a very good case. Royal Governor Tryon had the weight of authority. Both demanded support for the Brethren. The Moravians' neutral posture brought the wrath of both sides down upon them. But, as always in hard times, the Brethren fell back upon their faith, and survived. Their trials had only begun. Over the next decade they would look back to the days of the sixties and early seventies as times of comparatively carefree existence.

An early view of Bethabara, made from the God's Acre hill around 1760, reveals the triangular stockade erected in July 1756 during the French and Indian War. The two large structures within the fort are the Congregation House, right, and the Brothers' House. At the far left, outside the stockade, is the cluster of buildings that marks the original settlement. The cabin with a chimney is the hut found by the first Moravian settlers, while the long, low building is the first structure erected by them, the sleeping house. The brewery stands at far right, where the restored 1788

Gemeinhaus now stands. The stockade and the alert posture of its inhabitants were probably responsible for the survival of the Moravian settlement, as French-inspired attacks by Indians were commonplace in the surrounding countryside. The settlement at Walnut Cove was virtually wiped out, and a fatal attack occurred on Salem Creek near where South Main Street now crosses it.

Courtesy of the Moravian Archive,
Herrnhut, Germany

Bethania was founded in 1759 by a group of Moravians who chafed under the restraints of Bethabara's communal system and a group of outsiders who wished to live with them. The Moravians, John Beroth, Henry Bieffel, Gottfried Grabs, Balthasar Hege, Adam Kremer, Charles Opiz, Michael Ranke, and Christopher Schmidt, were assigned lots in the southern half, known as the Lower Town. The non-Moravians, George, Martin, and Michael Hauser, Philip Schaus, Frederick and Henry Schorr, Henry Spoenhauer, and John Strup, took up lots in the Upper Town. Gottfried Grabs and his family moved into the first cabin, marked by "B" on this 1761 town plan. In less than five years the population of Bethania had equalled that of Bethabara. Much of the old road to Bethabara, at upper right, is still in use today, although a section near the midway point is now on private property.

Courtesy of the Frank Jones Collection

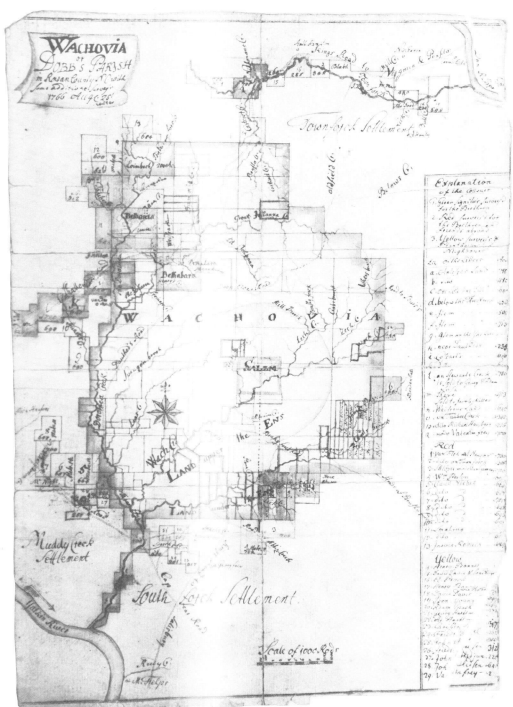

In 1766, Gottlieb Christian Reuter drew this map of Wachovia and included surveys of some of the Moravians' neighbors' property. The road that enters at the upper right and exits at lower left was known as the Great Wagon Road or the King's Road and stretched from Pennsylvania to Salisbury. It was down this road that the first Moravian settlers came to their new land in North Carolina. Clustered along the road and the Town Fork Creek to the north are the lands of such early non-Moravian settlers as Benjamin Young (19), David Davis (18), and Henry Banner (14), while to the northwest is the 684 acre tract of Jarvis Roebuck (13), listed as a "friend abroad." To the south, property owners are Adam Spach (20), George Hartmann (21), Adam Hartmann (22), Christian Stauber (23), John Mueller (25), and Valentin Frey (29). Wachovia received its second name from the fact that Governor Arthur Dobbs, in 1754, granted the Moravians special status politically so that they might not have to deal so directly with the outsiders who ran what was then Rowan County.

Courtesy of the Frank Jones Collection

The first house erected in Salem, completed in January 1766, was intended only as a temporary quarters for the workmen who would build the town. It endured, however, for 140 years, until it fell down of its own accord in 1907.

Courtesy of the Frank Jones Collection

Around 1760, Joseph Williams came from Virginia to the Yadkin River Valley. A few years later he married Rebecca Lanier and built this substantial house in the Panther Creek watershed, near the present Lewisville. Williams fought with the colonial forces in the Revolution, attaining the rank of colonel, and fathered eight sons, all of whom became men of distinction in North Carolina and other areas of the new nation. His youngest son, Nicholas, managed the plantation, where he produced "Old Nick" whiskey, a brand that became nationally known before statewide prohibition halted distilling in 1908. One of Nicholas' sons married the daughter of Tyre Glenn, whose magnificent plantation house still stands across the Yadkin River in Enon. The Williams homesite was noted for its elaborate formal gardens, including a number of magnificent boxwoods, and much of the original plantation remains today in the hands of the Williams family, although Colonel Williams' house was destroyed by fire in 1885.

Courtesy of Historic Winston

Each year the gravestones in God's Acre are given a good scrubbing in preparation for the Easter Sunrise service. Here the first grave, that of John Birkhead, a Yorkshireman who died in 1771, receives careful treatment.

Courtesy of the Frank Jones Collection

Under pressure from their neighbors to declare for or
against the British crown, the residents of Salem
desperately sought a way to remain neutral. After
hours of painstaking deliberation, they issued this
statement on February 15, 1776. Careful wording of
all their public utterances would serve them well
during the years of war to come.

Courtesy of the Frank Jones Collection

We the Subscriber, Inhabitants of the Towns of
Salem, Bethabara, & Bethany in the Parish of Dobbs
for our selves, and our fellow Inhabitants of
said Towns, hereby solemnly promise and
declare, that in the present calamitous
Circumstances of North America, which
we heartily pray to God Almighty, in
his Mercy soon to avert. We intend
to demean our selves as hitherto
as quiet people, who wish the Welfare
of the Country and Province, and that
we, not either of us, will not at any
Time intermeddle in political Affairs,
and that we will chearfully assist, and support the Country along with our other fellow
Inhabitants in paying of Taxes and any
Thing else, that is not against our Conscience
and our Privileges upon which we have settled
here, and that we in no Case whatever shall or
will do any Thing that shall detrimentall
to the good Province we inhabit

Salem this 15th Day of Febr: 1776
Mich: Graff: Lor: Bage.   Gottfried Grabs

Conflict and Revolution 1773-1783

By the time of the War of Regulation, a considerable population had established itself in the countryside surrounding the Moravian towns. To the southwest, in the west bend of the Yadkin, Joseph Williams had taken up a land grant covering thousands of acres, and while the land was being cleared for the town of Salem he began building a plantation house in the watershed of Panther Creek. To the north of Panther Creek, along the river, other plantations were sprouting. The Conrad brothers, first Christian, then Johann and Isaac, had begun arriving around 1765, taking large land holdings west of what is now Vienna.

Farther to the north, between the Conrads and the old Indian village, were arrayed such landowners as Martin Armstrong, sheriff of Surry County, his brother John, a captain of militia, and Alexander Martin, a lawyer who would later be governor of North Carolina. Justice of the peace Gideon Wright lived nearby. Wright and the Martin-Armstrong axis had long been at odds with each other. When Surry County was carved from Rowan, Wright had managed to have the courthouse sited upon his land near the river, but following a series of questionable maneuvers, the right to the courthouse had been wrested away by the Armstrongs and Martin and moved to their land at Richmond. The personal and political differences between these factions would bode no good for the Moravians.

Walkertown, to the east, had been a hotbed of dissidence during the Regulator uprising, with one of its residents, Sam Wagner, being denied a pardon by Governor Tryon, despite the atmosphere of amnesty that prevailed in the aftermath of the Governor's victory. In the same area, Thomas Linville, Sr., and his son had been building up their original four hundred acres since the year of the Brethren's arrival in Bethabara.

Around these large landholdings others had begun to gather, putting up homesteads, the beginnings of outlying towns. The trade brought to Salem by these outsiders contributed greatly to the prosperity of the Moravians, but, as usual, they had to take the bad with the good. It was known far and wide that the best brandy in the piedmont could be had at the Salem Tavern, and not a few of the visitors drank past any reasonable capacity. To the chagrin of the peaceful Brethren, fights often broke out on Main Street, sometimes involving three or more combatants at once, and the occasional sound of gunfire was not unknown. But the cash still flowed, and there was little that the Salemites could do but stand by and pray for the souls of the wicked. For those of their own who might stray in the same direction, a quiet warning from the Collegium was usually sufficient.

The bad feeling aroused in the area by the Moravians' neutrality during the War of Regulation was not helped by what the neighbors took to be overbearing self-righteousness. With relations already tense, word began to filter down from Massachusetts and Pennsylvania of great doings. A battle for freedom was brewing. If the king and his parliament would not listen to the voice of America, why then, the Americans would rise up and throw off the royal yoke. The residents of Wachovia took in this news with trepidation. They might not like it, but they paid their taxes. The English had done them favors, first declaring their sect a bona fide ancestor of the Anglican Church to give them official status for migration, and later, creating Dobb's Parrish for them, that they might maintain better control of their self-governing system. Besides, there was the matter of their rent. They still had to pay 150 pounds per year to an English landlord. If they supported the patriot cause and it lost, the English would take their land. The patriot leaders were not hesitant to make it clear that the reverse could also be true.

Once again, the Moravians found themselves in a squeeze. And once again they fell back upon their indomitable faith. Painstakingly they put together a statement defining their neutral position. With the royal government in virtual exile in the east, their rebellious neighbors pressured the new continental government to have the Moravian lands confiscated. Accusations were leveled at them by both sides. They would not accept the Continentals' paper money. They were harboring spies. They were demonstrating disloyalty to those who had helped them to escape the persecutions in Europe. They were profiteering, making fortunes from the sacrifices of the patriot cause. They did what they could. But they found, as did their Quaker neighbors in Guilford County, that nothing was enough.

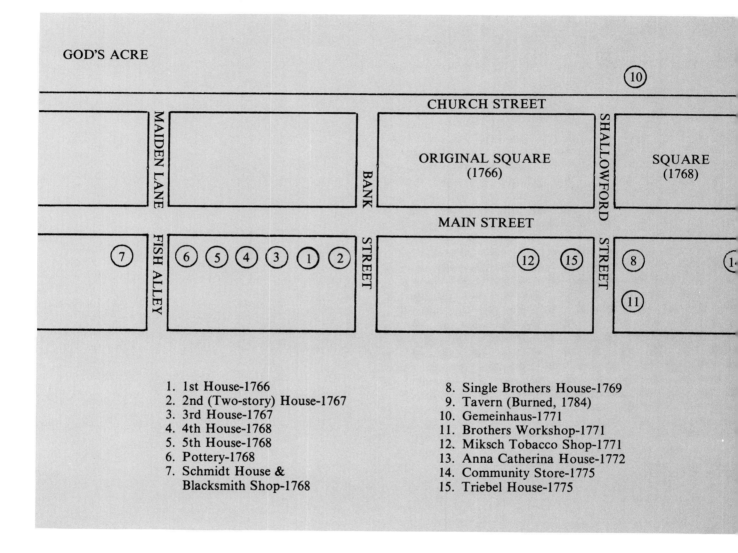

GOD'S ACRE

CHURCH STREET

MAIDEN LANE

SHALLOWFORD STREET

ORIGINAL SQUARE
(1766)

SQUARE
(1768)

BANK STREET

MAIN STREET

FISH ALLEY

⑦ ⑥ ⑤ ④ ③ ① ②   ⑫ ⑮   ⑧ ⑭
⑩
⑪

1. 1st House-1766
2. 2nd (Two-story) House-1767
3. 3rd House-1767
4. 4th House-1768
5. 5th House-1768
6. Pottery-1768
7. Schmidt House &
   Blacksmith Shop-1768
8. Single Brothers House-1769
9. Tavern (Burned, 1784)
10. Gemeinhaus-1771
11. Brothers Workshop-1771
12. Miksch Tobacco Shop-1771
13. Anna Catherina House-1772
14. Community Store-1775
15. Triebel House-1775

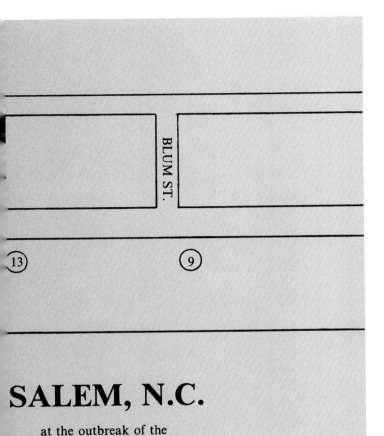

SALEM, N.C.

at the outbreak of the
Revolutionary War

*Map by Fam Brownlee
Art by Steve Smith*

The real sticking point was that the Moravians had set themselves a higher ideal than was common, and, conformity being the prized virtue that it is in America, their neighbors objected. All the blame cannot be put upon those neighbors. The Brethren were right to stand firm upon their beliefs, but there had, perhaps, been more pious tongue-clucking then some people could take.

In the midst of all this disharmony, the Brethren suddenly found themselves at odds from within. As a means of avoiding enforced military service, the Moravians had agreed to be triply taxed. The inflation caused by the almost worthless Continental money, which they had also been forced to accept, made itself felt most harshly upon the backs of the single brothers. For some time they agitated vigorously for an increase in wages and prices. When, in 1778, the Collegium finally granted some increases, they found themselves faced with the first labor union in Wachovia. Declaring the amount of the increases not enough, the single brothers walked out. Beginning a tradition that lasts to the present, this first labor union failed. The Collegium also began a tradition that would be applied in labor disputes in later years—steamroller tactics. Threatened with expulsion from Wachovia, the brothers took the proposed increase and went back to work.

Despite such internal squabbles and the constant pressure from outsiders, the faith of the Moravians prevailed. Not even a visit by Lord Cornwallis himself could upset the scheme of things. He dashed into town in pursuit of Nathaniel Greene, creating a considerable stir, but in the end the most memorable moment came when one of his men made off with a Bethania lady's cooking pot. In the Wachovian tradition of perseverance and thrift she pursued the culprit and returned with her property well in hand.

The American Revolution was one of the Moravians' low points. It is, therefore, easy to understand their jubilation when it was finally over. As strange as it might have seemed to some of their neighbors, the residents of Salem were the first people in the newly independent nation to hold an official July the Fourth celebration. Again, the Brethren were victims of misapprehension. Their celebration had little in common with current practice. Theirs was a celebration of peace, not victory. They had survived. Their land was intact. And in this wonderful new country, founded upon ideals of freedom and justice, perhaps, at last, they would be left alone to pursue their own interests.

In 1788, those Moravians who had decided to remain in Bethabara built the church which still stands as the centerpiece for Historic Bethabara Park. The building was a substantial one, with a sanctuary and organ loft in the east end and living quarters in the other. It is the oldest remaining Moravian church in the Southern Province. At the left is a house erected by a member of the Schaub family.

Courtesy of Bill East

A Village of Tradesmen and Craftsmen 1784-1848

If they thought to be left to their own pursuits, the Brethren were sadly mistaken. For a while, at least, they were spared the reality of the situation.

With the return of peace, trade flourished and there was time for more humanistic endeavor. The music of the serious Moravian composers was reaching its peak and Johann Friedrich Peter, John Antes, and Johannes Herbst were among those whose works enhanced the music being played and sung in Salem. On May 31, 1791, the new President passed through on his grand tour of the South and was exposed to the best that Moravian culture could supply. Characteristically, he was more interested in pedestrian concerns, praising the neatness of the village and the functional niceties of its waterworks.

Marshall, to whom the Salemites owed so much, died in February 1802, leaving a gap that would not be filled for almost ten years. With the arrival of Lewis David von (later de) Schweinitz in 1812, Moravian culture in North Carolina reached its high point. De Schweinitz was born in Bethlehem, Pennsylvania and educated in Europe, becoming probably the first American-born person to receive the doctor of philosophy degree. In Salem, he took Marshall's former position in the church and served capably for ten years. But he is better known for his work in botany. Having published his first scientific treatise as a student, he continued his work in Wachovia, and in 1818 presented his synopsis of North Carolina fungi before the prestigious Society of Naturalists in Leipzig. Following publication of numerous other works, his *piece de resistance* was presented in 1831 before the American Philosophical Society in Philadelphia. *The Synopsis of North American Fungi* detailed 1,203 species and several genera of plants discovered by de Schweinitz and is a major work in the field of science.

De Schweinitz was held in such esteem outside the Moravian community that he was offered the presidency of the University of North Carolina, which he turned down, stating that his duties with the church were more important. In 1822 he returned to Bethlehem. Despite the later contributions of his descendants, his loss was sorely felt in Salem.

The Moravians needed all of the leadership that they could find, for a new era of trouble was upon them. As early as 1765, when Dr. August Schubert left Bethabara because of his objections to the communist system, there had been some rebellious sentiment within the community.

On the morning of January 31, 1785, Salem's first tavern, erected in 1771, burned to the ground. Because it offered no place for visitors to spend the night, it was often necessary for one of the local citizens to give up his bed to an outsider. Accordingly, material and funds already appropriated for construction of a house for the single sisters was diverted to construction of a new tavern, two and one-half stories tall with vaulted cellars for the storage of food and drink. In 1791 George Washington would pause here on his grand tour of the South, spending two nights at the Moravian inn. Two fire engines were ordered from Germany and arrived by overland wagon from Charleston in May. They were among the first mechanical firefighting devices in America and, certainly, the first in North Carolina. The engines were kept in a house especially built for them on the west side of the square and saw their first action in August 1786 when they were used on an overheated smokehouse behind the tavern. At least one of them would still be in use when Henry Shaffner's home became, in 1863, the second dwelling in Salem to burn, making a remarkable record of only two residential fires in nearly a century.

Courtesy of Bill East

Constructed in 1790, this building would later serve as the Salem Calaboose.

Courtesy of Bill East

By the turn of the century, discontent had grown, particularly among the younger residents. The diaries are liberally sprinkled with warnings issued by the Collegium to this or that brother, and even a sister or two. The best known of these malcontents was Van Neman Zevely. An orphan and an outsider, he was taken into the church in 1798 and quickly became the best cabinet maker in town, also caring for the water works. His troubles at first were trivial. In 1803 he was twice warned about keeping a horse outside of town. Then he was asked to take over the cabinet making shop and refused, because he was making more money on his own. Threatened with expulsion, he acceded to the Collegium's demands, but he did not like it. The Collegium branded him a "rabble-rouser" and warned that he would be expelled if his deportment did not improve.

Expulsion came up again in 1806 over some trouble with a girl from Bethania. Zevely professed innocence, but was severely reprimanded and sent to work as a missionary among the Creek Indians. Working away from the constant control, he was happy and even became a member of Salem's Congregational Council. But bigger trouble was on the way.

He fell in love with Johanna Sophia, daughter of Christian Gottlieb Shober, the biggest landholder in Wachovia. Despite Shober's reluctant endorsement, the church refused the pair permission to marry. Zevely's offer to move out of Salem while remaining an *auswartige* (outside) member was also rebuffed. The young lovers went ahead with their marriage and suffered expulsion, moving to Shober's paper mill on the Petersbach. Shober's influence finally gained them reinstatement, as *auswartige* members, and in later years Zevely became one of the best known and most devoted of the Moravian missionaries. But he had bucked the establishment and he was not alone. Another young brother, Thomas Christman, finding Salem's system stifling, moved north of town, founding the community of Liberty, from which the present Liberty Street draws its name.

Those who protested found encouragement from outside. For the first thirty years the Moravians had maintained a religious monopoly that extended beyond the boundaries of the Wachovia tract. But by the 1780s the disciples of John Wesley had begun to appear on the fringes of the Moravian settlement.

24

Around 1755, John Alspaugh built a house on Muddy Creek near what is now Clemmons and began laying the foundation for the Methodist Church in the area. By 1775, with the assistance of George McKnight and John Douthit, Jr., he had a thriving Methodist congregation organized at Hope. To the north John Doub, a tanner from Bethania, built a house near the present Pfafftown and began holding Methodist services there. Over the next century his descendants would dominate Methodism in the western party of the county. In short order, Concord Methodist Church (1780) was begun near the Yadkin, and Love's Methodist (1791) and Bethlehem Methodist Episcopal (1800) began operating near Walkertown. In 1807 the Mount Pleasant Church, which still stands overlooking the Tanglewood golf course, began a 122 year active course.

In their usual fashion, the Moravians considered soberly the threat posed by this invasion of outside thought, and determined to do nothing about it. They might lose a few of their members who were weak in faith, but that might be a good thing for a congregation to which faith was so important. The losses amounted to more than a few, but the Moravians ignored them. They had a town to finish.

In January 1798 they laid the cornerstone for Home Church. Brother Zevely spent many hours with Brother Bachman, sent down from Lititz, working on the casing for the organ. The church was consecrated in 1800, and two years later the school for little girls set upon a new era when it began accepting non-Moravian boarding students.

There were minor setbacks. In 1803, and again in 1814, many inhabitants were stricken with measles. Not a few died. But there were also minor triumphs. In 1806, Brother Eberhard modified the town clock to make it strike the quarter hours. That year, too, John Vogler opened his jewelry and silversmith shop, beginning a family business that would last 167 years. About the same time, Charles F. Bagge built a storehouse on the road to Friedland, the first building in what would become known as Bagge or Charles Town, and later, Waughtown.

Traugott Bagge lived in the community store until 1787, when he built this house across the street at the corner of West and Main. The original structure of chipped stone was stuccoed and outlined to give the appearance of cut stone, while the faces of the upper half-story retained their original brick surfacing, also being outlined. The frame addition was built in 1821. Although demolished in the 1930s, the house has been reconstructed by Old Salem, Incorporated.

Courtesy of Bill East

Salem's first fire engine, acquired in 1785.

Courtesy of Bill East

By the middle of 1815, Bagge, along with John Christian Blum and Emanuel Shober, had established Salem's first real bank, a branch of the Bank of Cape Fear. In an era in which many banks failed, the Cape Fear, despite disasters such as the burning of thousands of dollars worth of currency, survived and even flourished, providing an omen of the direction that Salem's economic interests would take in the twentieth century.

As the town grew, so did the range of interests. The Moravians were, in the beginning, opposed to slavery, but not for the usual moral reasons of the abolitionists. First, having others to do one's work would promote laziness, even slothfulness, within a system that pivoted upon industrious behavior. Second, black Africans represented another possible intrusion by outsiders. Their ways would not be the ways of the Brethren. But the infamous institution could not be avoided. Following a brief period of absolute prohibition, the church allowed, under certain well-defined conditions, the rental of slaves from neighboring establishments. Inevitably, some of these blacks became fixtures in the community.

The Brethren's treatment of slaves could not have been popular with their neighbors. The Sunday school founded by the Female Missionary Society taught reading and writing, which would, in later years, violate the provisions of the Black Codes. But the Moravians' tradition of education for all was strong, and they persevered.

They could not avoid, however, being drawn more and more into the mainstream of life in America. In 1831 the long-standing freedom from military service, granted to the Brethren of Unity by Governor Dobbs before the Revolution, was rescinded by legislative enactment. With their usual sense of history, the Moravians formed a volunteer company on July 4 of that year. But the traditions of the settlers of Wachovia were gradually being broken down. By 1860 many of the basic ones would be gone, and residents of Salem would own nearly three hundred slaves.

By 1787, when this watercolor view from the southwest was made by Ludwig Gottfried von Redeken, Salem was a thriving center of trade, revolving around the Single Brothers' House (1769/1786), near the center of the picture. Clustered behind the Brothers' House, on what is now Academy Street, are the Brothers' workshop, woodhouse, and teamsters lodge. Directly across the square is the Gemeinhaus (1771). Next, to the right, facing on Main Street, is the community store (1775), then, facing on Church, the Single Sisters' House, completed the year before the painting was done. From foreground to background, the next three buildings are the Anna Catherina house (1772), the Traugott Bagge house (1787), and the Tycho Nissen house (1782). At the far right is the tavern (1784). Clustered along Main Street to the north are the first group of dwelling houses built in Salem (1766-68) and the pottery (1768). In the foreground at the left is the Single Brothers' tannery/brewery complex and buildings to support the satellite farms.

Courtesy of Old Salem, Inc.

Home Church, begun in 1797 and completed in 1800, capped the first flurry of building in Salem. It was designed by Frederick William Marshall. In June of that year, the bell, a 275-pounder cast in Bethlehem, Pennsylvania in 1772, was moved into the tower. Ten years later, the Inspector's House, at center, was built across from the church, facing on the square. Additions were made to it in 1838 and around 1850. To its left can be seen the foundation of the former Boys' School housekeeper's house (1811) and a portion of the Boys' School (1794). The photograph was taken shortly after the Civil War.

Courtesy of the Frank Jones Collection

John Christian Blum was appointed, in 1815, as an agent of the Bank of Cape Fear, the first real bank in Salem. In 1827, he began operation of a printing shop to supplement his income from the bank. Later that year, following the disappearance of some ten thousand dollars in currency which brother Blum claimed had been accidentally burned up, his association with the bank was terminated and he began, in 1828, publication of *Blum's Almanac,* the orange covers of which still grace newsstands throughout the South. The following year, he published the first edition of the *Weekly Gleaner,* the first local newspaper. Apparently, his temperament fitted the work. It is said that he was once interrupted on the job with the information that one day's weather had been omitted from the Almanac. "Give them snow and hail" he stormed, without looking up. Naturally, on the appointed day, northwestern North Carolina got one of its biggest snowstorms ever.

Courtesy of Bill East

Two of Salem's earliest industries were carried on in these buildings on Shallowford (Academy) Street near the present intersection of Marshall. Here such hides as could be had in trade were tanned and beer was brewed for sale in the tavern. The local brew never attained the level of fame enjoyed by that made in Bethlehem, which received favorable comment from George Washington, a connoisseur who made his own, but it rivalled the famous brandy made by the Single Brothers in popularity at the tavern.

Courtesy of Bill East

In 1791, George Washington found Salem's most impressive attribute to be its water works, powered by gravity from a spring located near the present Calvary Moravian Church. The water was conducted to cisterns in the town by a conduit of hollowed out logs. In the 1820s Salem expanded and modernized its original system, and in 1828 constructed the first overshot water wheel pump in the area. The pump sat at a spring in the ravine east of Bank Street, powered by water brought around a hill from two miles away in a wooden trough. The spring water was pumped uphill over a hundred feet to a supply cistern at the south end of Cedar Avenue, and flowed thence by gravity through glazed terra-cotta pipes to about a dozen other cisterns strategically located around the town. For the next half-century this system would adequately serve Salem's needs.

Courtesy of Bill East

The Salem Cotton Manufacturing Company was formed in 1836 with Francis Fries, who, with Dr. Schumann, had dabbled in cotton milling, as its head. Fifty thousand dollars were subscribed, and the following year a brick building incorporating steam driven spindles and looms was completed and operations begun. Mr. Fries resigned as president in 1840 to found a wool-carding concern, and through a combination of bad management and the panic brought on by the Mexican war, the Salem Cotton Mill went under in 1847. The building was bought, in 1854, by John M. Morehead of Greensboro and converted into a grist mill, and was operated as such by him and his successor, Rufus L. Patterson. During the Civil War, Robert Gray and Peter Wilson reconverted it into a yarn mill, which soon failed. The Fries family reacquired the building in 1877 and operated it again as a grist mill for some time. The original structure, having undergone several renovations, stands today on Brookstown at the foot of Cherry and is used as a warehouse by a transfer company.

Courtesy of Bill East

When he left, in 1840, the Salem Cotton Manufacturing Company, Francis Fries began a modest wool-carding operation on the New Shallowford Road (Brookstown Avenue), between Salt (Liberty) and Elm (Trade) Streets. A year or two later he added spinning and hand looms for manufacture of Salem Jeans. By 1846 his brother Henry W. Fries was a partner, and the building at left was being used as the woolen manufactory of F. & H. Fries. Rapid expansion followed, and in 1848 the brothers added onto the complex a cotton mill to supply the woolen mills with warp. Further improvements in the business produced this building, shown in the 1870s before the construction of the Arista Mill.

Courtesy of Bill East

The Salem pottery, established in 1768 on Main Street, would have, in its seventy-five year life, only three master potters, Gottfried Aust, formerly master in Bethabara (1755-1771), from 1771 to 1788, Rudolf Christ, another former Bethabara master (1786-1789), from 1789 to 1821, and John Frederic Holland, from 1821 until his death in 1843. Henry Shaffner came, in 1833, to serve as apprentice under Holland, but did not like his master. He set up his own shop, shown here, in the old builder's log house, the first structure in Salem, in 1834, later turning the business over to Daniel T. Crouse, who continued the business until his death in 1903. Henry Fries Shaffner, grandson of Henry Shaffner, operated a pottery for a brief time around 1890 at the rear of his father's drug store on the original pottery lot.

Courtesy of the Frank Jones Collection

For its first year-and-a-half of existence, the new county town had no official name, and was generally referred to as Salem. But in January 1851 the General Assembly passed an act naming the town after Major Joseph Winston. Major Winston, born in Virginia in 1746, came to North Carolina in 1769, settling on the Dan River in that part of Surry County that would later become Stokes. He had gained fame as an Indian fighter during the French and Indian War, and would be honored for his bravery against the British at such battles as King's Mountain and Guilford Courthouse. After the war he served several terms in the State Senate and the United States House of Representatives. Some years after his death in 1815, his remains and tombstone were placed on the battlefield at Guilford Courthouse National Military Park.

Courtesy of Bill East

A County Town and Civil War   1849-1869

In their first century in North Carolina the Brethren had lived in four different counties. They had purchased their land in Anson County, but before they could get a house put up they were living in Rowan. By the time Salem was beginning to look like a town they were in Surry (1770). And before George Washington could get by to have a look at their part of his new realm, they were in Stokes (1789). The county seat had always been at a comfortable distance. But by the 1840s, the Democratic domination of Stokes' affairs had become troublesome to the conservative Whig businessmen and industrialists of Salem. They began agitating in Raleigh for formation of a new county, in which they hoped to gain control of the decision making process.

On New Year's Day, 1849, they got it, and with it, a pack of trouble. Stokes was cut in two and the southern half, ironically named Forsyth, after a former resident of the northern half, needed a county seat. Salem, due to its size and location, was the logical site.

The elder Brethren were horrified at the thought. They had always joked that no trip to Hell could be worse than a visit to Richmond, when that town was the county seat, and when Richmond had been blown off the face of the earth by a "cyclonic wind," they had exchanged knowing looks and fingered certain passages in their Bibles.

A county seat meant courts, with their attendant whipping posts, and the church abhorred corporal punishment. Worse, the inevitable hangers-on that congregated during court sessions often tended to drink far past their capacities, whereupon the hurrahing and punching and shooting began. It was already bad enough at market time. So the church offered to sell the county commissioners a parcel of land known as Double Bottoms, near the present Ogburn Station, for a courthouse site. Salem's leaders in commerce saw that such a move meant the death of their town and arranged a compromise.

The church agreed to sell the commissioners 51¼ acres lying directly north of Salem for a new county seat. The price was five dollars an acre. In return, the commissioners agreed that the whipping post would not be visible from any point in Salem. That was not enough for some. A small group of Moravians emigrated to Iowa that year.

When the town lots were put up at auction on May 12, 1849, Robert Gray bought the first one, number forty-one, at the corner of Third and Main, for 465 dollars. In the center of the block facing the courthouse he built this two-story frame house and in the next few years became widely known as one of Winston's early business leaders. On the corner, where the Government Center now stands, he built a brick store, while also operating the Wachovia Steam Flour and Paper Mills on Peter's Creek, where the Winkler Motor Lodge now stands at the corner of Academy and Peter's Creek Parkway. On March 17, 1882, a year after Mr. Gray's death, his home burned to the ground and was replaced by the building known as the Gray block.

Courtesy of Mrs. A. H. Galloway

The first public schoolhouse in Winston stood on lot number one, at the northwest corner of Liberty and First, as stipulated in the deed made by the Moravians to Forsyth County commissioners. The frame structure, built in 1847, housed all ages of children, and was the first public building in Winston. One of the early teachers there was Mrs. Eliza W. Kremer, whose term of duty encompassed the Civil War years and afterward. In the 1880s the school was torn down to make way for the Brown and Williamson Tobacco Company's new buildings. Like so many historic places in Winston today, the site is now a parking lot.

Courtesy of Bill East

The new town, called for the time being Salem, acquired an instant resident, lawyer Thomas J. Wilson. He had been living in the country north of Salem, leasing his land from the church, and when Salt (Liberty) and Main Streets were extended into the new town and cross streets laid out, he found himself living on the northwest corner of Main and Second. He got a special deal, paying only 133 dollars for his lot. On May 12 of that first year, when the remaining lots were put up at public auction, Robert Gray had to pay 465 dollars for the first lot sold, number 41, at the southwest corner of Main and Third Streets.

Until the new courthouse could be completed, court was held in the Salem concert hall. The first big case tried there was that of two young Wesleyan missionaries, Adam Crooks and Jesse McBride, arrested in Salem and charged with distributing abolitionist literature. They went on trial at the October 1850 session of Forsyth Superior Court. The concert hall was packed with spectators, many of whom were crying for blood. Crooks was freed, but McBride was convicted and sentenced to receive twenty lashes, stand in the pillory for one hour, and serve one year in the county jail.

Released pending appeal in May 1851, McBride was seized by a mob near Colfax and threatened with being hanged. He chose to leave the state. A month later Crooks was dragged from the pulpit of Lovejoy Chapel in Montgomery County by another mob. Soon thereafter he, too, left. Needless to say, the peace-loving Moravians were glad to witness the opening of the new courthouse.

By the end of the second year, the county seat was beginning to take on the appearance of a town. Near the courthouse, the jail was nearing completion. Salem's *People's Press* said of that building: "May the mere sight of its grated windows prove a terror to evildoers and its cells remain tenantless." There were homes, the first built by Jesse Kennedy at 138 Liberty Street, two hotels and four stores operated by Robert Gray, Sullivan and Bell, William Barrow and Harmon Miller, who opened the first one on Fourth Street across from the courthouse. At the corner of Liberty and Seventh stood the church, completed in 1850, of the Methodist Protestants. A block south at the corner of Sixth, the Methodist Episcopal congregation had begun construction of their Winston Station Church. They held services in the courthouse until the building was completed in 1856.

In January 1851 the General Assembly finally gave the two-year-old town a name of its own, Winston, after Colonel Joseph Winston of Revolutionary War fame. That same year, John Panky opened a boarding school and Winston's first post office was established, with John Vest as postmaster.

By the mid-1850s, the two towns had their first daily stagecoach service on the Raleigh to Salisbury route. Trade possibilities were further enhanced in 1854 by the completion of the Fayetteville and Western Plank Road through Salem and Winston to its terminus at Bethania. F. & H. Fries built an adjunct to it that ran by their mill on New Shallowford (Brookstown).

The new county town generated a kind of excitement that contrasted sharply with the sedentary nature of Salem. The legal business that emanated from the courthouse attracted men of ambition, both in trade and in politics. Any event that was not a daily occurrence could draw enormous crowds for so small a town. Popular attractions were militia drills and the big church meetings. A brush-arbor revival would bring in throngs that choked the streets with big city traffic.

But the biggest attractions were the court sessions and elections. Then the covered wagons would roll in from all parts of the county and the merchants laid on temporary clerks to handle the flow of fresh produce, dairy products, and dried fruits and berries that the country people offered in barter for ready-made shoes, cloth, and household utensils. Big court sessions brought in the medicine shows, where snake-oil doctors hawked their wares, and now and then a traveling menagerie might appear, with its scruffy Brazilian parrots and perhaps a lion, or a once-graceful gazelle. Aspiring politicians stalked potential voters in the camp grounds near Liberty and Fourth, and on Second between Main and Church. There, fiddles and banjos could be heard into the wee hours.

Political rallies brought more organization to the amusements. In October 1852 the local Chippewa Club held a big rally for the popular General Winfield Scott, Whig candidate for the presidency, and his running mate, William A. Graham of North Carolina. Speakers were chosen for their staying power and the enormous crowd must have been ravenous from the smells of cooking by the time they were allowed to eat. Over a ton of barbequed meat was served up, with Brunswick stew and country style vegetables. The

Designed by Francis Fries and completed in 1851, Forsyth County's first courthouse reflected the then popular Greek revival in architecture. Its Greek porch was twelve feet wide, the porch roof being supported by four thirty-foot Doric columns. The building itself was of red brick, forty-four by sixty feet, facing on the south side of the square. The courtroom was on the second floor, with the ground floor divided into six offices, two being rented to attorneys, while the others were occupied by the clerk of court, sheriff, register of deeds, and the grand jury. The courthouse functioned as Winston's first civic center, playing host to church and political meetings, literary lectures and dramatic presentations, as well as serving as the center for July the Fourth celebrations and other public occasions. The building was torn down in 1896 to make way for a more commodious structure.

Courtesy of Bill East

following month, Scott and Graham were humiliated at the polls by Franklin Pierce, a mild and inept New Englander. From then on, the town of Winston voted with the Democrats.

The conservative Salem Whigs took a dim view of their Democratic neighbors. But the old town was deep in the throes of its own revolution. Many did not like it, but times had changed, and Salem had to adjust or perish. The ritual of the lot was done away with as an unwieldy anachronism in a world where decisions had to be based upon logic and made with dispatch. Americans spoke a form of English, and to facilitate communications the Moravian Church dropped German as its official language in 1855, finally catching up with the thinking of Marshall. The following year the communist lease system was abolished. That same year the town was incorporated. The elected officials, mayor Charles Brietz and such commissioners as Edward Belo, Francis Fries, and Rufus L. Patterson, were progressives. Amid much hand-wringing, Salem found its way into the modern world. But for those who clung to the old ways, worse, much worse, was to come.

While the Moravian elders fought their losing rear-guard action against the intrusions of the democratic process, Henry Clay and other Southern congressmen were fighting another losing battle against the swell of Republicanism in the nation's capital. With the election to the presidency, in 1860, of Abraham Lincoln, everybody's world came apart. Where Jesse McBride and Adam Crooks had been, in 1850, merely a nuisance, the new order in Washington threatened old principles that many southerners would not give up.

The early months of 1861 were a time of mass meetings and bitter arguments. At one point, the largest crowd ever seen in these parts gathered around the Winston courthouse to heatedly debate the pros and cons of secession. John W. Alspaugh, publisher of the *Western Sentinel* in Winston, was a rabid secessionist, while L. V. Blum of Salem's *People's Press* was unionist to the core. They exchanged insults in every edition. In the conservative tradition of the Moravians, North Carolina was one of the last states to leave the Union. But by spring young men were drilling near the courthouse. Mexican War veteran Joseph Masten was the drillmaster. On May 21, 1861, North Carolina seceded, and the next day the first company, the Forsyth Rifles, elected Alfred Belo, son of the builder of the Belo House, as its captain. Two

days later Rufus W. Wharton formed the Forsyth Grays. As the two companies prepared to leave for the war, Captain F. P. Miller put together a third, the Forsyth Southrons.

On June 17, the first two companies boarded wagons for Danville, Virginia, where they became a part of the Eleventh Regiment of North Carolina Volunteers under Colonel W. W. Kirkland. It was a festive occasion, but barely a month later, after the first battle of Bull Run, Second Sergeant Samuel C. James would write home that he would "be well content to see a peace made and us ordered home tomorrow, and I am only expressing the sentiments of all the boys in the company." Already, Forsyth had its first casualty, Private Henry Butner, who died of typhoid fever, not Yankee bullets. Despite the yearnings of Sergeant James and his comrades, the war went on to become the bloodiest and most hurtful conflict that this country would ever fight. And the young men of Winston and Salem would suffer some of the worst of the blood and hurt.

The number of local boys in uniform grew. Captain George Stowe's Forsyth Volunteers became Company I of the Thirty-Third North Carolina Regiment. Others served in Company G, Second North Carolina Battalion and Company K, Forty-Eighth North Carolina Regiment. A group from Salem became the Twenty-Sixth North Carolina Regimental Band, under Captain Samuel T. Mickey. James E. Mann, pastor of Winston's Methodist Episcopal Church, became a captain and led Company D of the Fifty-Seventh North Carolina Regiment.

Medical services were desperately needed. Frank Shaffner of Salem, who began as a private in the Eleventh, was soon a surgeon in the Fourth North Carolina Regiment. S. D. Davis, who lived near Bethania, left his private practice to serve in various staff capacities. By January, when Henry Bahnson, the seventeen-year-old son of Salem's Moravian Bishop, volunteered for service, the twin towns had been stripped of the cream of their young men.

The neighboring counties supplied their share. The Yadkin Grey Eagles, Captain Reuben E. Wilson commanding, served under Rufus Wharton in the notorious First North Carolina Battalion, Sharpshooters. And from Davie came Company E, Forty-Second Regiment, under command of Captain Thomas J. Brown, who would later build the first tobacco warehouse in Winston. Among the Walkers,

The Belo House on Main Street in Salem was built from 1849 to 1860. It later served as the Salem Home for aged and infirmed people and orphan children, under the auspices of the King's Daughters. Today it provides a pleasant retirement setting for senior citizens.

Edward Belo was a man of enterprise. Trained as a cabinet maker, he quickly deserted his craft for the merchant trade. He set up a store in his father's home, the former "skin house" on Main Street at the corner of Bank. In 1849 he purchased the property from his mother, and the adjoining tract, that of his brother Lewis, and began a new building. Soon afterward "E. Belo's Leviathan: The Universal Depot and World Renowned Emporium" opened for business, the store occupying the first floor on Main Street. The second

floor, facing on Bank, was the family residence, and the third would eventually house the legion of clerks employed in the enterprise. The ornate grillwork and the iron animals were made in Belo's foundry outside the town.

Edward Belo became a man of substance in the community and later took an interest in the new town of Winston, being one of the founders of the Wachovia National Bank and the Roanoke and Southern Railroad, which he served for a time as president. His son Alfred founded a great newspaper empire in Texas after the Civil War and was an intimate of President Cleveland. Other Belo descendants achieved distinction of their own extending into the middle of the twentieth century.

Courtesy of Bill East

Wards, and Cuthrells in that company we find the name of Spencer Hanes, who would assume command upon Brown's promotion to Major.

These men walked out of a spring morning into a winter of disaster. The carnage was terrible. Captain Wharton was captured while hunting in Virginia, and Henry Bahnson met the same fate at Gettysburg. They were the lucky ones. Ephraim Transou had brought his sons home to Pfafftown from Texas to serve the South. In less than a year three of them were dead in battle.

Wharton's Sharpshooters were almost wiped out at Winchester. Captain Jesse Atwood of the Forty-Eighth was killed during the battle of the Seven Days and his brother, B. F., fell along with Hurtz and Augustin Butner and Sandy Petree at Antietam Creek. John Barrow, brother of the letter writing Henry, was wounded at Fredericksburg, where J. C. Stafford and Henry Banner were killed.

Probably the hardest suffering of all was felt by the men of the original companies in the Eleventh Volunteers. After reorganization as the Twenty-First North Carolina Regiment, this unit fought and left its blood upon nearly every major battlefield of the eastern theater. At Second Bull Run, Albert Alspaugh, Newton Doub and Hart Newsome were wounded, while Lieutenant Colonel Saunders Fulton, the regimental commander, and Captain W. F. Brown were killed. Another of Henry Barrow's brothers, David, was wounded at Second Bull Run, and Charley Clauder, whose brother wore the Yankee blue, fell at Chancellorsville, where their leader, the remarkable "Stonewall" Jackson, was mortally wounded.

The holding of command in the Twenty-First was a dubious distinction, Colonels Kirkland and Fulton having already fallen in that role. Now it claimed more victims, first at bloody Antietam Creek, where Captain Frank Miller died, and then at Cedar Creek, in the Shenandoah Valley, where the valiant and pious William Pfohl fell. Under Drewry's Bluff on the James River near Petersburg, Sam James, now a captain, was killed while commanding under the dashing P. G. T. Beauregard. A few months later, James' son-in-law would die in the hospital at Greensboro of an illness contracted while serving in eastern North Carolina.

If the listing of casualties makes the war seem grim, it still does not suffice. It was worse. When Captain James took command of Company L, Twenty-First North Carolina, in 1863, he found only twenty-two men capable of going into action, in a company that had begun with more than one hundred on its rolls. And at Appomattox, barely a hundred, from over a thousand who had marched off to First Bull Run, answered the Twenty-First's final roll call. Young Henry Bahnson called the war "the abomination of desolation." None of his comrades would disagree.

Belo's pond was the site of the mill and foundry of Johann Frederick Belo, father of Edward, and was located north of town near the present Belo Street. There the Winston Water Supply Company, a privately owned concern, constructed in 1880-81 the first water works to serve the town of Winston. The community that grew up in the area became known simply as "the pond," and would later lend its name to a famous semi-professional black baseball team, the Pond Giants.

Courtesy of Bill East

But there were moments of triumph, as at First Bull Run when the Yankees turned and ran, inciting panic in the streets of Washington, and in the string of lightning victories with Jackson in the Shenandoah Valley. The Twenty-First was there at the apex of the Confederate campaign when they seized, for a few moments, the crest of Cemetery Hill at Gettysburg. But when they were driven off they left behind Major Alexander Miller, son of Winston's first storekeeper. He was mortally wounded by a round from a Union cannon and died sometime later, having received tender care from a Union family.

Perhaps the most futile victory of all was Henry Bahnson's moment of glory. Near Farmville, Virginia, after the fall of Richmond, Bahnson and a few others captured over a hundred Yankee prisoners, winning praise from their commander. Two days later Bahnson himself became a prisoner for the second and final time in the last fight near Appomattox, when General Gordon, defiant to the end, finally laid down his arms.

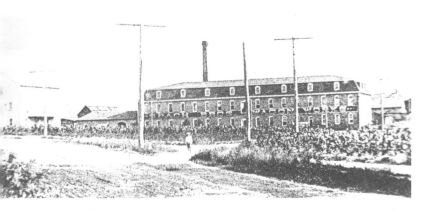

The Spach family began, in 1854, the manufacture of wagons. By the turn of the century, J. C. and S. L. Spach were operating the "Spach Bros. Wagon Works" in Waughtown. They cut the timber for their products in winter, when the sap was down, to insure against "worms and sun-cracks," then seasoned it for three to five years to eliminate any possible warpage. The wheel hubs were made from white oak, specially treated to prevent shrinking or cracking. When the coming of the automobile reduced the demand for horse-drawn vehicles, the Spach company evolved into the Unique Furniture Company, which endures to this day.

Courtesy of Sam Dalton

If life at the front was grim, life at home was little better. The Fries Cotton and Woolen Mills ran around the clock, turning out cloth for uniforms, blankets, tents, and coats. Robert Gray's paper mill slowed to a crawl as rags were taken for bandages. Courageous women, among them Mary Clewell, Laura Vogler, and the public schoolmistress Eliza Kremer made the dangerous trip to the camps carrying food and medicine for the troops in the field. There were shortages of everything, especially metal, paper, and salt. Constant complaints were made against the distillers, who many thought were guilty of misappropriation of corn.

The Salem Female Academy flourished as parents in the battle zones shipped their daughters to the supposed safety of the Moravian town, but there were not enough beds. Inspector Robert de Schweinitz and Steward Augustus Fogle found their ingenuity taxed to the limit in finding supplies of food. The Governor forwarded occasional windfalls from captured Union stockpiles.

As the war expanded and conscription became universal, desertion reached epidemic proportions. Union sentiment in Salem proved an attraction for men on the run from the army. Most who passed through Winston and Salem did so peacefully, begging a handout if they could before moving on toward the hills. But some came in groups and, in the latter stages of the war, heavily armed, threatening the defenseless citizens if they were not quick enough to produce a bit of meat or some cornbread. Many figured them to be worse than any Union army might be.

Thus, when General Palmer's cavalry, a part of Geneal Stoneman's raiding party, entered the area the day after Lee's surrender at Appomattox, the citizens offered no opposition. In Winston, H. F. Burke made a valiant but futile charge up Liberty Street, his pistol blazing. He hurt no one, and when the Union troopers made in his direction, he quickly reversed himself and disappeared. In Salem a Confederate battle flag appeared from an upper window of the Academy and an unlady-like rebel yell was heard, but in their haste to obtain supplies, Palmer's men overlooked this indiscretion. Little was taken in either Winston or Salem, but upon leaving, some of Palmer's men exchanged shots with a little band of die-hards at the Shallow Ford, and some looting and destruction of property took place in neighboring Davie County.

But the war was over and most of the survivors came home. Alfred Belo went west with the idea of joining Nathan Bedford Forrest in his proposed guerilla campaign and ended up founding a publishing empire in Texas. Henry Bahnson, alternately walking and hitching rides on the railroad, returned to Salem. Charles Davis, who had left his half built house near

Belews Creek only to be captured and sent to Indiana, was too sick to make the long trip. He bought army surplus equipment and set up a blacksmith shop. A year later, his health restored, he left Indiana, bringing with him his Yankee forge, anvil, and bellows. He finished the house, which still stands. The towns of Winston and Salem, left, with the rest of the South, in economic ruin, needed such determined souls to begin the rebuilding process. Many of the young men who would have lent their hands and minds were no longer available.

In 1941, the state erected this historical marker at Bethania, designating the Western Terminus of the Fayetteville and Western Plank Road. The road, completed in 1854, entered Salem from High Point and crossed into Winston before turning northwest to its final destination. The toll ranged from a half-cent per mile for a man on horseback to four cents for a six horse team. Maintenance was expensive, and, despite the stiff five dollar fine, many users succeeded in avoiding the toll by riding around collection points. Eventually the road company went out of business. In 1858, the *People's Press* reported that "The plank road leading out west, by Fries' factory and the Wachovia steam mills, has been improved by removing the plank and macadamizing it."

Courtesy of the Frank Jones Collection

The Salem gas works was established in 1858 at the northeast corner of New Shallowford (Brookstown) and Elm (South Trade) Streets. The gas, manufactured by running hot resin over pieces of heated limestone, was intended primarily to light the F. & H. Fries mill, located a few feet to the northeast. The surplus was piped into local homes and industries. The black byproduct, dumped into a nearby stream, gave its name to "Tar Branch." The gas works was made obsolete by the arrival of cheap electric power in the 1880s and went out of business around 1897.

Courtesy of Bill East

On May 21, 1861, North Carolinians reluctantly joined the rest of the South in seceding from the Union. The next day, the Twin City's first company was formed. Alfred H. Belo was elected captain. In Virginia the company became Company D, Eleventh North Carolina Volunteers (later the Twenty-First North Carolina Regiment, State Troops). Above the company is seen in camp, drawn up for inspection, but the scene below was more common. Like all soldiers in all wars, the boys from Winston and Salem soon found that the biggest enemy is always boredom.

Courtesy of Bill East

Despite the distinguished gunsmiths that Salem produced, the Moravians were never known for their skill in using firearms. But their music was justly famous, and it is fitting that one of their best known contributions to the Confederate cause was a group of musicians known as the Twenty-Sixth Regiment Band, photographed on their first furlough. Left to right: James M. Fisher, Second B♭ tenor horn (substituting for A. C. Meinung, who was ill); Julias A. Leinbach, E♭ bass, later second cornet; Daniel T. Crouse, first B♭ tenor horn; Augustus L. Hauser, first E♭ alto horn; William H. Hall, second E♭ alto horn; Joe O. Hall, second B♭ cornet, later bass; A. P. Gibson, first B♭ cornet; and Samuel T. Mickey, captain and E♭ cornet. Others not present were H. A. Siddell, Julius A. Transou, Charles Transou, Edward

Peterson, D. J. Hackney, W. A. Reich, and W. A. Lemly. Mr. Lemly would later become president of the Wachovia National Bank and W. A. "Gus" Reich, the drummer boy, achieved fame as a magician, "The Wizard of the Blue Ridge," and, in his capacity as a tinsmith, made the casket for the famous "Siamese Twins." William Hall was captured in the retreat from Gettysburg, and Augustus Hauser was the only band member to die in service. Tenor hornist Daniel Crouse became, in the 1870s, Salem's last master potter.

Courtesy of the Moravian Music Foundation

On September 21, 1869, James A. Gray, son of Robert Gray, married Aurelia Elizabeth Bowman, and following their honeymoon, took her into this new brick house that he had built on Main, a few hundred feet below his father's store. According to the memoirs of their daughter, Bess Gray Plumly, James told his new wife that he had been undecided whether to build on Main or on the corner of Fourth and Cherry Streets. "Oh," she replied. "I'm so glad you didn't build way out there, for I would have been afraid of the wolves and other wild animals." She may have been exaggerating slightly, but the proposed site, where Stith's store now stands, was definitely a place for country living in those days.

The house had a parlor with walnut furniture, including a marble-topped table and a Morris chair, and a carpet with a lovely floral design. Bess remembered the carpet well, she said, because that was where the "whippings" were meted out. There were two white servants, a cook and a nurse, and a long porch across the back of the house, at the end of which stood a great rarity of the day, an indoor toilet. The location of the house was ideal, for after Mr. Gray joined the Wachovia Bank as its first cashier, he had only to walk next door to get to work. In 1882, however, he built his magnificent new house on Cherry Street and moved his family there.

Courtesy of Mrs. A. H. Galloway

The Twin City has never been known as a hotbed of literary creation. Although drama critic Bosley Crowther received his formative education in the local public schools, Winston-Salem's sole claim to home-grown literary talent rests upon the frail shoulders of the poet John Henry Boner. Born in Salem in 1845, Boner's verse was, from the beginning, influenced by the romantic output of the Charleston poets, as epitomized by Henry Timrod. For a time during Reconstruction, Boner edited the *Salem Observor,* expressing therein his radical Republican sentiments in a continual journalistic battle with George Mathes' *Western Sentinel.* Abuse, and threats of worse, led him to give up the paper and leave Salem. In 1883 his first volume of verse, *Whispering Pines,* was published, and four years later he went to New York, where he served as associate editor of the prestigious *Literary Digest* and literary editor of the *New York World* and the *Century* dictionary. But he fell into dire financial straits, and his health began to fail; first he lost the use of his hands, then was struck by chronic bronchitis. Finally, in 1803, he died of "consumption," tuberculosis, in Washington, D.C. His birthplace, immortalized in his poem, "Cricket Lodge," has been preserved by the restoration of the Lick-Boner house in Old Salem. In 1954, *Whispering Pines* was reprinted by John Blair.

Courtesy of Old Salem, Inc.

The tranquil aspect of Salem's Main Street in 1866 belies the tension and desperation of the times. A. B. Chaffin's Salem Hotel, originally the tavern dining rooms (1816) is at left. Continuing up Main Street toward Winston, the buildings are: the Blum house (1815), the Samuel Schulz (shoemaker) house (1819), the Christoph Vogler (gunsmith) house (1797), and the John Vogler house (1819). Continuing past the intersection with West Street, we find the community store (1775), the Salem Post Office, originally the Temperance Hall of the Young Men's Missionary Society and the Sons of Temperance (1849), and the Single Brothers' house (1769/1786). All but the post office, which was demolished in 1961, and the Blum house have been restored by Old Salem, Incorporated.

Courtesy of Old Salem, Inc.

When the Civil War ended, the Moravians had more than peace to celebrate. Despite the loss of some of Salem's finest young men and the desperate economic situation in the community, in 1866 the Home Church was decorated, and festivities commenced to commemorate the centennial of the founding of the village. The centennial text came from Isaiah, the same source as was used on the day that the felling of trees began for the building of the house of peace.

Courtesy of Bill East

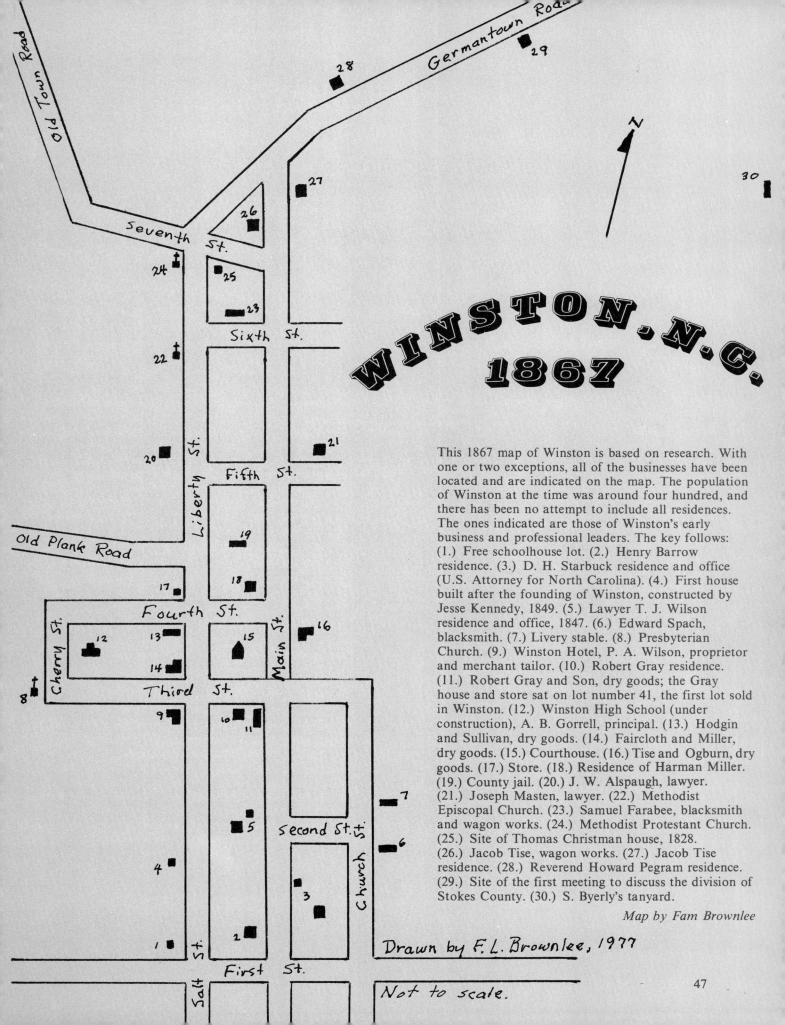

WINSTON. N.C. 1867

This 1867 map of Winston is based on research. With one or two exceptions, all of the businesses have been located and are indicated on the map. The population of Winston at the time was around four hundred, and there has been no attempt to include all residences. The ones indicated are those of Winston's early business and professional leaders. The key follows: (1.) Free schoolhouse lot. (2.) Henry Barrow residence. (3.) D. H. Starbuck residence and office (U.S. Attorney for North Carolina). (4.) First house built after the founding of Winston, constructed by Jesse Kennedy, 1849. (5.) Lawyer T. J. Wilson residence and office, 1847. (6.) Edward Spach, blacksmith. (7.) Livery stable. (8.) Presbyterian Church. (9.) Winston Hotel, P. A. Wilson, proprietor and merchant tailor. (10.) Robert Gray residence. (11.) Robert Gray and Son, dry goods; the Gray house and store sat on lot number 41, the first lot sold in Winston. (12.) Winston High School (under construction), A. B. Gorrell, principal. (13.) Hodgin and Sullivan, dry goods. (14.) Faircloth and Miller, dry goods. (15.) Courthouse. (16.) Tise and Ogburn, dry goods. (17.) Store. (18.) Residence of Harman Miller. (19.) County jail. (20.) J. W. Alspaugh, lawyer. (21.) Joseph Masten, lawyer. (22.) Methodist Episcopal Church. (23.) Samuel Farabee, blacksmith and wagon works. (24.) Methodist Protestant Church. (25.) Site of Thomas Christman house, 1828. (26.) Jacob Tise, wagon works. (27.) Jacob Tise residence. (28.) Reverend Howard Pegram residence. (29.) Site of the first meeting to discuss the division of Stokes County. (30.) S. Byerly's tanyard.

Map by Fam Brownlee

Drawn by F. L. Brownlee, 1977

Not to scale.

47

Francis Fries was Salem's first real industrialist. Before
the founding of the Salem Cotton Mill in 1837, he had
dabbled in textiles in partnership with Dr. Frederic
Schuman, but it was not until 1840, with the opening
of his woolen mill on the New Shallowford Road, that
he began to achieve real success. He was also a civic
leader, becoming, in 1849, chairman of the first
Forsyth County board of commissioners and of the
Court of Pleas and Quarter Sessions. He was born in
this house. When he died in 1863 his brother and
partner Henry W. Fries was there to carry on the Fries
industrial empire.

Courtesy of Bill East

Industrial Revolution and Expansion 1870-1913

Winston and Salem generally escaped the worst ravages of reconstruction. The influence of the Moravians was strongly felt in this matter, as they had consistently promoted good relations with the blacks in the area. The majority of the newly freed slaves that settled around the two towns became solid citizens, serving mostly in such roles as domestic workers and general laborers, although small businesses began to appear from the first. Men of religion were the early leaders in the black community and when, in 1871, the St. Paul's Methodist congregation was formed, it became the center for social and political activities.

Before and during the Civil War, the number of free blacks in Forsyth County was insignificant. Slavery had come late to the northern Piedmont. In 1790 Peter Harston, with fifty-eight slaves, had been the leading practitioner of the infamous institution in the area. Joseph Winston's eighteen slaves made him one of the major traffickers in Stokes County. The Moravians and their friends in Wachovia held, that year, barely forty slaves among them.

By 1860 George Brooks, whose plantation lay along the Yadkin River north of the old Shallowford Road, was the top slaveholder in the county with a total of nearly one hundred. Isaac Gibson owned forty-two, and Constantine Banner held forth near Germanton with a force of twenty-five. The greatest increase had occurred, however, in the old Wachovia tract. F. and H. Fries owned forty-seven slaves for work in their mills. Other leading slaveholders among the Moravians were William Fries, twenty; John Reich, seventeen; Edward Belo, eleven; and Christian Hege, ten. Most of the "better" families in Salem had one or two house slaves. In Winston, Harman Miller had eight, William Holland, six, Rufus Patterson, five, and Robert Gray and Frank Gorrell four apiece. The number of slaves in Winston and Salem combined exceeded three hundred.

But the ratio of black-to-white was low compared with the eastern part of the state, where one family, operating the Orton Plantation near Wilmington, owned more than two hundred slaves. Little is known about the activities of blacks in Forsyth County during the Reconstruction years, but with the establishment of tobacco manufacturing in the 1870s, the need for cheap labor brought about a black population explosion in Winston. "Mr. Bill" Taylor, with his pre-work prayer meetings, inspired a certain loyalty in

many of his workers. R. J. Reynolds, who was known for his almost total dependence upon black labor, had strict rules about talking on the job, but singing was encouraged. Standard spirituals and work-songs from the slave years were prevalent, but Reynolds' workers were aware of their freedom as men. A *Harpers Weekly* correspondent reported the following "work song" from Winston in the early 1890s.

> Before I'd work for Reynolds, R. J.,
> I'd walk all night and sleep all day.
> Walk all night to keep from sleepin'
> An' sleep all day to keep from eatin'.

The members of Winston's black community were an industrious lot. By the mid-1890s, there were more than sixty local blacks involved in business and the professions. They operated fifteen restaurants, seven grocery stores and at least two barber shops. James E. Guy and K. H. and T. F. Hawkins were making shoes. There were eight teachers, seven ministers, three physicians, including Dr. H. H. Hall, Winston's first black doctor, and a lawyer, John S. Fitts. Albert Hill and S. A. Ratliff had forges in operation for ironworking. Mrs. Nannie Bethell, wife of the Presbyterian minister, operated a hotel in her substantial home at 135 East Seventh Street. Her daughter, Carrie, taught under principal R. W. Brown at the old Woodland Avenue School. George Hickerson operated a bus line and W. H. Gaines had a billiard parlor on Old Town (Trade) Street, between Fourth and Fifth Streets. There was a florist, Dave Harris; a plumber, Rufus Shouse; an engineer, Ike Wallace; and an undertaker, S. L. Long. M. P. Matthews, who lived in Blumtown, preceded George Black as a brickmaker. There was a cigar maker, Thomas Lindsey; a dye works, R. M. Johnson; and even a distillery, operated by Jim Wall at his home on Eighth Street. Aaron Moore headed the all black Hook and Ladder Company Number 2, located near the intersection of Seventh and Depot (Patterson) Streets.

And these pioneers took an active interest in politics. Between the end of the war and the beginning of the "Red Shirt" campaigns, Israel Clemmons, J. B. Hughes, J. B. Gwyn, Rufus Clemmons, G. L. Lattie, Henry Pendleton, and Henry Hargraves served as aldermen. Although there would not be another black

Mrs. Brilla Fansler's home, built some time after the Civil War, occupied what is now the site of the Reynolds High School Auditorium. It had three rooms and a dirt floor. The giant blackgum tree was cut down when the auditorium was built. Mrs. Fansler's apple orchard was located on the ground where the high school now stands. H. P. and Will Fansler and Charlie Wright, from left, posed for this 1904 photograph.

Courtesy of the Frank Jones Collection

alderman until 1947, these men and others demonstrated capable leadership, and this would prove helpful to both the white and black communities in the trying times to come.

When the soldiers came home in the spring of 1865, the economic situation was so bad that the Winston Board of Commissioners passed an ordinance providing that those who could not pay their taxes in cash might work out their debt on the city streets, with no penalty or stigma attached. In Salem, the Moravian church was almost penniless through loss on its investments. The citizens of Winston and Salem went diligently to work. The results were astonishing. By the end of the following year the cash flow was sufficient to support the opening of the first locally owned bank, the First National of Salem. But in 1867, the principal products of Winston remained wheat and dried fruits and berries. Local manufacturing was confined to the two wagon works in Waughtown, a textile mill and a carriage works in Salem, and the carriage and wagon works of Isaac Tise, S. H. Reniger and Jacob Tise in Winston. Robert Gray had taken over Gottlieb Shober's old Salem Mill, and, with steam power, was turning out several types of paper and flour. Tobacco manufacture in the twin towns remained strictly a cottage industry.

But an avalanche of change was in the making. The State Convention of 1868 approved a charter for the extension of the Northwest North Carolina Railroad from Greensboro to Winston and Salem. Under the direction of Henry W. Fries and Edward Belo, and with the assistance of the Richmond and Danville Railroad, which would later take over operations, the line was completed in July of 1873. When the first train chugged into the tiny Winston station, it brought with it the seeds of the industrial revolution.

Since before the war, James Ogburn had been putting up ten to twenty thousand pounds of plug at his home in the country, but Hamilton Scales began, in 1870, the first real tobacco manufactory in town, using a converted carriage house on Liberty Street. With the coming of the railroad, tobacco factories and warehouses sprouted like crabgrass all over town. From the curb-stone trade of Tom Jones and Robert Mosely in the early seventies, tobacco warehouse sales ballooned to over eight million pounds in 1878.

Other new industrial works began in milling, wood, and iron working, and older industrial concerns expanded. Winston became a boom town. In 1882 the first county fair was held in Brown's warehouse. The following year it got a formal name, The Forsyth County Wheat and Cattle Fair. By the time of that second fair there were more than twenty major tobacco manufacturing concerns in the county, with well over half of them located in Winston, and the town could boast of four big sales warehouses for the bright leaf of the piedmont.

All of this industrial activity had a sensational effect on the population. When the first tobacco warehouse opened in 1873, there were about six hundred people living in Winston. By the census of 1880, that figure had mushroomed to 2,854. Builders found themselves suddenly to be men of wealth as they scrambled to keep up with the demand for houses, factories, warehouses, and other assorted types of structures. They built two banks and two saloons, Apple and Rose, and Darius Morgan. The hotel industry failed to keep pace, there being only three in the town, and none of those much better than boarding houses. But Winston got its first private detective, Thomas Pfohl, who operated out of his general merchandising store.

Merchant's associations began to spring up, and their demands for improvements of streets and roads brought action. In 1890, Winston paved a portion of Main Street with granite blocks, while in the county, engineer Charles A. Reynolds was laying the first section of macadamized road in the area. By that time the railroad had been extended westward to North Wilkesboro, and a new line, the Roanoke and Southern, was operating to the North.

As more and more Salemites invested their energy and funds in the new industry, the two towns drew gradually closer together. Already they were referred to as Winston-Salem, or the Twin Cities, and in 1899 the two post offices were consolidated under one postmaster. Six years later, the leading citizens of Winston and Salem joined together to found the Associated Charities, predecessor of the Community Chest and United Fund. It was one of the first such organizations in the South, and, again, the Moravian tradition of brotherly love was an important motivating force. The following year, a group of leading black citizens founded the Winston Mutual Life Insurance Company, which quickly became a matter of pride among the citizens, black and white, of both towns.

The city was bursting at the seams. Winston's population had zoomed to more than ten thousand, while Salem's shot up to nearly four thousand. The Moravians had profitted by Winston's location on their northern border, although they had paid a price in the breakdown of some of their traditions. Most of them did not seem to mind too much. At least they had the consolation of knowing that they had exerted a civilizing influence upon the raw new town. Now Winston was, by itself, a city, with two railroads, twenty-six churches, including two Moravian congregations, five public and three private schools, and a hospital.

By 1913, Winston had a third railroad, a public library, its first Boy Scout troop, a Quaker meeting house, and a new Methodist Children's Home for orphans. The Forsyth County Highway Commission, North Carolina's first, was agitating at home and in Raleigh for better roads. Many citizens of Salem had established successful businesses in Winston, and the leaders of the two towns had been working together for some time to promote their mutual best interests. Time was ripe to sanctify the common-law marriage of the two towns.

The appropriate legislation having been passed, the citizens voted on the question of consolidation in March. That the old Moravian isolationist strain had not quite withered away is demonstrated by the result. In Winston the vote for consolidation was 75.5 percent, while in Salem it was only 63.2 percent. On May 6, the citizens elected O. B. Eaton of Winston as the Twin City's first mayor. The new aldermen were E. D. Vaughn, C. M. Cain, G. E. Webb, P. S. Bailey, N. D. Dowdy, and G. W. Edwards of Winston and H. F. Shaffner and Fred A. Fogle of Salem. Finally, on Friday, May 9, 1913, what had been true in practice for years became true in fact. The Moravian village of tradesmen and craftsmen and the county town of industrialists became the city of Winston-Salem. Other than getting the date wrong on the marker raised to commemorate the event, the consolidation of the two towns was brought off with a minimum of difficulty.

The citizens of the new city could look back upon 170 years of hard striving and dazzling success and ahead to even better times in a nation that was just beginning to utilize its seemingly unending resources. They took little note of the gathering thunder-storm of war building over their old homelands in Europe. That year the fire department took delivery of its first motor truck.

In 1873, Winston got its first railroad service. The original depot was the low frame shed at the left between First and Second Streets. Within a few years, the burgeoning population and industry of the town forced an addition that more than doubled the space available. Parts of the original buildings still stand below Reynolds Tobacco Company's factory number 256.

Courtesy of Historic Winston

The earliest view of the O'Hanlon corner, at Fourth and Liberty, evokes the rugged frontier spirit of early Winston. In the building at left, R. Moore opened the Winston Hotel, one of the town's first, before going into partnership with Mr. Griffin. The building was later acquired by J. F. Prather for his general merchandise business, with the second floor let out to J. A. Robinson, who published there the *Winston Leader*. W. S. Martin opened the first shoe store in Winston there in 1876. Next door stood the bakery of J. S. Black, who carried a supplemental line of groceries. Samuel H. Smith added to the traditional mortar and pestle symbol a second free-standing one, the eagle-topped barrel, in front of his drug store. Mr. Smith served as mayor of Winston in 1885 and later that year was appointed postmaster. Dick W. Howard's Family Grocery and Confectionary came next, followed by Winston's first United States Post Office. The entire block was destroyed by fire in the 1880s.

Courtesy of Bill East

William T. Vogler, descended from Philip Christoph Vogler, continued the family tradition of superlative craftsmanship with the opening of his jewelry business after the Civil War. In 1867 he constructed the store building at left center, on the square in Salem, and there operated the firm until 1879. The building is now occupied by the Old Salem Store.

Courtesy of Old Salem, Inc.

As Winston slowly expanded, business had to move away from the square. In 1870, G. W. Hinshaw opened his wholesale and retail grocery, Hinshaw and Company, on Fourth Street at the foot of Old Town (now Trade) Street. He later took as a partner Mr. Bynum, and when Mr. Bynum left, one of his salesmen, N. H. Medearis, by which time the firm was handling all types of general merchandise excepting millinery and clothing. Note the star-shaped sign, advertising a brand of guano used in fertilizing tobacco, and the stepping stones, which were made necessary by the constantly muddy, unpaved streets. Hinshaw and Medearis joined F. & H. Fries in sponsoring the first cattle and wheat fair in Winston. By then they had constructed a three story brick store, seventy by seventy feet, with two steam-driven elevators.

In 1906, Glen Williams of Panther Creek, a gentleman and liquor distiller, horsewhipped United States District Attorney A. Eugene Holton, a prohibitionist, on the street in front of this store. The incident was brought on by a dispute between the two over Federal tax stamps, and was the culmination of a feud of several years duration. The Hinshaw and Medearis site is now occupied by the Anchor Company.

Courtesy of Bill East

W. T. Vogler began in business as a watchmaker and
jeweler in Salem with his brother E. A. Vogler. In
1871 he broke away to form his own concern. Seeing
the beginning of the Winston boom as a chance for
expansion, he moved his business there, locating at
234 Main Street, across from the Merchant's Hotel.
Here he poses, at center, with his employees for a
Fourth of July photograph. Note his trademark, the
large clock on the sidewalk. When the firm closed its
doors in the early 1970s it was one of the city's oldest
and most respected businesses. At left is the Forsyth
5¢ Bank, and the pictures lining the doorway to the
right of Vogler's mark the entrance to S. E. Hough's
second floor photography studio. The next business is
that of Joseph Bevan, Sr., watches and jewelry, and
the striped awning marks the concern of Efird and
Brother, grocers and confectioners.

Photo by S. E. Hough

Taken in 1879, this photograph shows the west side of Main Street near the intersection with Third. At the left is the first home of Wachovia National Bank. Next door, Eugene E. Gray stands in the doorway of his law office. Then come the businesses of W. P. Ormsby, pianos, organs, and sewing machines; the weekly *Union Republican,* J. W. Goslen, editor; W. T. Carter and Company, dry goods and notions; George T. Foust, general merchandise; and M. Stein and Son, clothiers. On the corner, Robert Gray had rented his brick store to S. E. Allen, a dealer in hardware. Beyond the courthouse square, on the corner of Fourth and Main, can be seen the windows of Brown's Opera House, above Vaughn, Brown and Carter's hardware establishment. Within a few months, jeweler W. T. Vogler would move his business from Salem into the building occupied by Foust. Part of this site is now occupied by Winston's oldest skyscraper, the Government Center Building, while the area shared by the bank and Gray's law office is reserved for parking by the county commissioners.

Courtesy of the Wachovia Bank

In 1874, Richard Joshua Reynolds, who was selling tobacco products for his father out of Critz, Virginia, decided to break away and start his own tobacco manufactory. Attracted by the new railroad and sales warehouses in Winston, he purchased, on October 19, lot number 139, located between Chestnut and Depot Streets just below Second, of the expanding Winston tract. He paid the Moravian Church $388.50. No accurate pictorial representation is known to exist of the first plant he opened in 1875, but the above painting is thought to be a fair likeness of the "Little Red Factory," fronting on Chestnut Street. One hundred and fifty thousand pounds of plug were turned out that first year, and a series of additions begun to the original building.

Courtesy of Bill East

In 1876, the firm of Pfohl and Stockton, inspired by a
visit to the Centennial Exposition, constructed
Winston's first modern store building on the southeast
corner of Main and Third Streets. It was a three-story
iron-front building with an Italianate facade, and,
according to Henry W. Foltz, an employee at the time,
had the first phone line in Winston. Technically,
the line was long distance, consisting of a waxed string
and empty tomato cans, connecting Pfohl and
Stockton with J. E. Mickey's store in Salem, three
blocks to the south. Mr. Foltz stated that it was
"...actually possible to understand some words over
this distance...." When commercial canning put their
chief product, dried fruits and berries, in the shade,
Pfohl and Stockton, in 1886, folded. This photograph
was taken some time in 1877.

Courtesy of Bill East

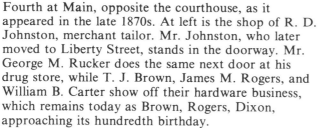

Fourth at Main, opposite the courthouse, as it appeared in the late 1870s. At left is the shop of R. D. Johnston, merchant tailor. Mr. Johnston, who later moved to Liberty Street, stands in the doorway. Mr. George M. Rucker does the same next door at his drug store, while T. J. Brown, James M. Rogers, and William B. Carter show off their hardware business, which remains today as Brown, Rogers, Dixon, approaching its hundredth birthday.

Courtesy of Bill East

John Francis Shaffner graduated from the Jefferson Medical College, Philadelphia, in 1860. After service in the Civil War, he began practicing medicine and soon was operating a retail drug business in this building at the corner of Fish Alley and Main Street. Later, he opened a cotton gin and boning mill at the intersection of New Shallowford (Brookstown) and High Streets. Burned in the 1880s and rebuilt, the mill building eventually became a part of the Briggs-Shaffner complex.

Photo by Fam Brownlee

Dr. Bahnson shows off one of his famous "Victoria Regia" plants in the lily pond behind his house in 1892. The white blossom is at the center surrounded by five circular petals. The Wilmington *Messenger* reported that the little girl was twelve years old and weighed sixty-five pounds, and that the largest petal measured sixty-six inches in diameter. The "Victoria Regia" was discovered in the upper Amazon and named for Queen Victoria. Dr. Bahnson's specimens are thought to have been the first grown outdoors in North Carolina.

Courtesy of the Frank Jones Collection

Henry Bahnson, too, survived the Civil War. Around 1880, J.S. Broadway stationed himself near the corner of Bank and Church Streets in Salem and captured Dr. Bahnson's house on film. Originally the Steiner house (1823), it had been modernized by the addition of a recessed entry way, containing an interesting second story porch, but the ornate brickwork on its chimneys was an antebellum legacy. The house has now been restored to its original configuration. To the right stood the home of the Reverend Edward Rondthaler, pastor of Home Moravian Church and, later, Bishop of Salem. Dr. Rondthaler's *Memorabilia of Fifty Years*, with appendix, published in the mid-1920s, serves as a valuable research tool for modern historians. The house, built in 1841, is known as the "Bishop's House." To its right can be seen the house for retired ministers (1816), since demolished.

Photo by J. S. Broadway

This view of the Steiner house (1823) in the 500 block of Church Street in Salem was taken from the east in 1878. At the time, the house was occupied by Dr. Henry Bahnson, whose famed "lily pond" was located near the bottom of the stairs.

Courtesy of Old Salem, Inc.

Joseph Renard operated this combined florist and grocery store at the northwest corner of Main and Fish Alley in the 1870s and 80s. He advertises the "best lamp oil" at twenty cents the gallon.

Courtesy of the Frank Jones Collection

This view of Salem College was taken in 1873 from the front of the old Boy's School. Main Hall, at the left, was built in 1854, replacing the 1771 Gemeinhaus. To the right of it is the building that housed the Girl's Boarding School, built in 1805. At the extreme right can be seen a portion of the Single Sisters House (1786 to 1821).

Sister Elizabeth Oesterlein began the school for girls in Salem in 1772. In May of 1804 the first boarding students, four girls from Hillsborough, arrived on campus. After over sixty years of distinguished service, the Salem Female Academy was granted, in 1866, a charter as a full-fledged college, but the first senior class, six in number, did not graduate from Salem College until 1879. Occupying its pleasant campus in the midst of the Old Salem restoration, Salem Academy and College can look back upon a history spanning nearly 175 years.

Courtesy of Bill East

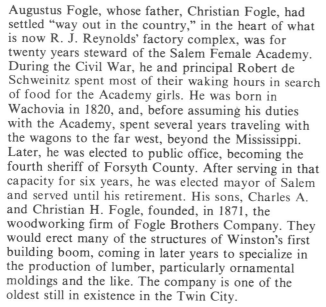

Augustus Fogle, whose father, Christian Fogle, had settled "way out in the country," in the heart of what is now R. J. Reynolds' factory complex, was for twenty years steward of the Salem Female Academy. During the Civil War, he and principal Robert de Schweinitz spent most of their waking hours in search of food for the Academy girls. He was born in Wachovia in 1820, and, before assuming his duties with the Academy, spent several years traveling with the wagons to the far west, beyond the Mississippi. Later, he was elected to public office, becoming the fourth sheriff of Forsyth County. After serving in that capacity for six years, he was elected mayor of Salem and served until his retirement. His sons, Charles A. and Christian H. Fogle, founded, in 1871, the woodworking firm of Fogle Brothers Company. They would erect many of the structures of Winston's first building boom, coming in later years to specialize in the production of lumber, particularly ornamental moldings and the like. The company is one of the oldest still in existence in the Twin City.

Courtesy of Bill East

One of the early engines of the Richmond and Danville Railroad streams slowly out of the Winston station in 1880. E. E. Harris is the engineer at the left.

Courtesy of Bill East

Looking west on Belews Creek Street at Depot
(Patterson) about 1880. At left is the Fogle Brothers
lumber yard and office. The first house on the right is
the newly built home of Sheriff Augustus Fogle. The
other two houses were occupied by Mary Parrish and
William F. Clayton. The ghostly horse and buggy are
a result of the slow film emulsion of the day, the
image having been only partly formed before the horse
was driven away.

Courtesy of Bill East

From the tower of the courthouse in 1891, Winston's
first major residential area can be seen spreading out
to the southwest. The intersection of Third and
Liberty Streets is in the foreground, and at right is the
First National Bank building, constructed in 1890.
Today it houses the Mother and Daughter store, but a
savings and loan institution covets the site for another
parking lot. Across the street is the town's first hotel,
the Winston, which was operated by P. A. Wilson in
the 1860s. It was later purchased by R. J. Reynolds,
and a portion of it used to entertain his business
colleagues. The extreme left portion of the building
was a saloon, operated by E. Loper. Next on Liberty
is the Twin City Hospital, Mrs. J. O. Hall, matron,
which began operation in 1887 in the former home of
Martin Grogan. The street running diagonally across
from the left is Second Street, and leads to Cherry. On
the northeast corner, at 203 Cherry, stands the home
of Mrs. M. C. Benton, built in the 1870s. Across the
street from her, with the tower, is the second home of
James A. Gray, at 134 Cherry, erected in 1882. Within
ten years of the date of this photograph the West End
had become Winston's fashionable neighborhood, and
the exodus had begun, paving the way for what is
today Winston's most disagreeable industry, parking
lots.

Courtesy of the Frank Jones Collection

The James A. Gray home at 134 North Cherry in
1886. The lot extended from Cherry all the way to
Marshall. The Downtowner Motor Lodge was erected
there in 1966.

Courtesy of the Frank Jones Collection

The residential properties in the Fourth-Cherry complex were soon filled up, and building began to move west on Fourth, spilling over onto Fifth Street as well. By the late 1880s, H. D. Poindexter had built his frame house, left, at the corner of Spruce and Fifth, and across the street, Dr. Robah F. Gray was living in the brick structure on the right. Dr. Gray's house was torn down in the early twenties to make way for the present First Baptist Church. Poindexter's home, one of the few remaining on Fifth Street, is an exact copy of wagonmaker J. G. Huff's house in East Bend in Yadkin County.

Courtesy of the Frank Jones Collection

Typical of the houses built along West Fifth Street in the 1880s and early 1890s is the home of John G. Young, coal and insurance broker, erected by Fogle Brothers in 1892. Mr. Young stands on the porch at left. His daughter, Lila, peeks from near the big tree, while John G., Junior, and daughter Terrell occupy the steps. Mrs. Lucy Wingfield Young is almost obscured by the potted plants at right. Terrell, who taught Sunday school for many years at Centenary Methodist Church, is one of Winston-Salem's most valued assets, as her accurate remembrances bring alive for us the days of yesteryear.

Courtesy of Terrell Young

About the time that R. J. Reynolds' first factory went into production, Calvin H. Wiley began an often discouraging eight year campaign to bring graded schools to Winston. Finally, in 1884, he saw his dream come to fruition with the opening of the Winston Graded School, the first such school in North Carolina. Julius L. Tomlinson was the superintendent and the roll for the year boasted more than 250 students. Mr. Wiley went on to become the most progressive State Superintendent of Schools in the South, and the school he had helped to found became the alma mater of most of Winston's business and civic leaders over the next half century. As the city built more schools, the name was changed to the West End School, and still later it served as office space for the city school administration. In 1946, the West End School was demolished to make way for the new Sears, Roebuck Department Store. A few years afterward, Mr. Wiley's home on Spruce was destroyed by the Piedmont Publishing Company for another parking lot.

Courtesy of Bill East

Salem tinsmith J. E. Mickey maintained, in the late 1800s, a farm at this pond that came to bear his name. George Black, the brickmaker, took his first job here in 1889. He was ten years old. The site is now a middle-class residential area, flanked by Bowen Boulevard and Attucks and Eldora Streets. Mr. Black lives in a house on Dellabrook Road overlooking the place where he cooked, sewed, and cleaned in the days before his handmade bricks brought him fame.

Courtesy of Bill East

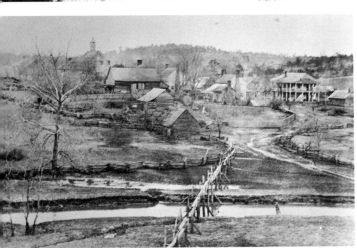

The tobacco boom had little effect on Bethania, the second Moravian town in Wachovia. This view, taken around 1880 from a hill to the southwest of the village, reveals a sleepy southern community at peace with the world. The dominant buildings are the church, at upper left, begun in 1806 and completed in 1809, and at the right, the two-story general store of Herman Butner and Eugene Lehman, built in 1836. The other principal business in the town was Christian Lash's general store, out of the picture at upper left. To the left of Burner and Lehman's store stands the two-story frame dwelling of Martha Butner Sides. At the upper center is another two-story frame house, constructed by Joseph Transou. Behind the barn is the Herman Butner house, and next to it the home of his partner, Eugene Lehman. Farther out to the left, along the road to Tobaccoville, stood the 1841 plantation house of Dr. Beverly Jones, designed by the famous architect Dabney Cosby, who had earlier designed some of the buildings of the University of North Carolina and the governor's mansion in Raleigh. The old Fayetteville and Western plank road, which had its western terminus near the Butner and Lehman store, was long since out of service by the time of this photograph, but the plank footbridge across Muddy Creek, in the foreground, appears to be in good working order.

Courtesy of Old Salem, Inc.

In 1882, D. H. King came from Richmond and began selling ice and coal in Winston at the corner of Third and Depot Streets, above. His coal yard is shown below. He later added a soda fountain, one of Winston's finest, on Main Street across from the Merchant's Hotel. In 1887, he built a bottling works on Water Street, where he bottled mineral water and flavored sodas as well as Vienna Cabinet and Tivoli beer.

Courtesy of Historic Winston

When Messieurs Pfohl and Stockton erected their store in 1876, behind it, on the corner of Church at Third, stood Lash's tobacco warehouse, the second in Winston. By 1883, they had built the brick warehouse at left and taken over operation of Lash's. The addition to the warehouse on the right was built with material taken from T. J. Brown's original building.

Courtesy of the Frank Jones Collection

Major T. J. Brown, having survived the Civil War, came to Winston from Davie County in 1872 to find Major Hamilton Scales' tobacco manufactory already in operation. G. W. Hinshaw remodelled a stable on Liberty Street near Scales' building and Scales opened the town's first tobacco sales warehouse. The success of the venture brought forth capital, and a second warehouse was erected later that year on Church Street between Third and Fourth. Finally, in 1884, Major Brown, in partnership with W. B. Carter, erected this building on Main Street, between Fourth and Fifth. The sales floor had eighteen thousand square feet of space, and the building was valued at twenty thousand dollars. No known picture exists of the first two warehouses, the second of which was operated in the 1890s by the Farmers' Alliance formed to oppose the Tobacco trust.

Courtesy of Historic Winston

Pleasant Henderson Hanes, in 1872, left his sales position with Brown & Brother in Mocksville and began the manufacture of tobacco products in Winston, with his brother John Wesley as partner. Their first factory burned in 1877, and soon thereafter they rebuilt on Chestnut Street between Second and Third Streets. As their business expanded, they built the pictured structure, factory number 223, in front of the other on Church Street. By the mid-1880s, P.H. Hanes and Company's "Mammoth Tobacco Works," turning out such popular brands of plug and twist as "Missing Link," "Man's Pride," and "Greek Slave," was the largest tobacco manufactory in Forsyth County. Around 1900 the Hanes brothers sold out to R. J. Reynolds' portion of the tobacco trust for nearly half-a-million dollars and went their separate ways in the textile industry.

To the right of Hanes' factory can be seen the livery stable and horse and mule trading establishment of Smoak and McCreary, and beyond it, the First Baptist Church building on Second Street. Behind the Hanes' building, on Church Street, is the tobacco factory of W. T. Gray and Company, while in the foreground along East Fourth Street can be seen the saloons of George Roediger and C. C. Shoffner. The blank space near the center was the site of T. J. Brown's second tobacco warehouse, later used by the Planter's Alliance in 1891. The warehouse burned in the early 1890s. Part of the Gray and Hanes buildings is still being used today by the R. J. Reynolds Tobacco Company.

Courtesy of Reynolda House

While tobacco turned Winston into a boom town, Salem was not standing still. The successes enjoyed by F. & H. Fries triggered a burst of growth, and the town expanded into West Salem, as is evident from this view taken in the 1880s, looking northeast from near the present intersection of Broad and West Streets. The F. & H. Fries complex is near the center of the picture, the building with the tower being the flouring mill, built in 1837 and in use today as a warehouse. To the right is the Arista Mill, constructed in 1880, the first mill in the South to have electric lights. In the grove of trees to the left of the mill stand the homes of William Blair and John W. Fries, still occupied by their descendants. At right is the intersection of Academy and Poplar Streets, and in the left foreground can be seen one of the famous Fogle toilets.

Courtesy of the Frank Jones Collection

The Farmers' Warehouse was established in 1881 by a partnership including G. W. Hinshaw, E. M. Pace, and Colonel A. B. Gorrell. Colonel Gorrell later assumed control of the business and brought in his sons, Robert W. and Peter A. Gorrell. The site, Trade between Fourth and Fifth, is now the area from the Mall Cinema to the far end of the McCrory Department Store.

Courtesy of Historic Winston

By 1880, F. & H. Fries had outgrown their old mill. That year they began the Arista cotton mill, across the street next to the original Wachovia Cotton Mill (1837), which they had acquired and were operating as a grist mill. The new mill was a three-story brick building with a two-story pyramidal-roofed stair tower, and with its 6,480 spindles and 180 looms cost 125 thousand dollars. It was the first factory in the South to have electric lights, the current being supplied by a gas generator. Fuel for the generator was supplied by the gas works at lower right. The two mill buildings still stand and are currently being used by the Lentz Transfer Company.

Courtesy of the Frank Jones Collection

In the 1830s, Henry E. Meinung began making carriages in Salem. He took on Eugene Alexander Giersch, who would remain with the firm for half a century, as his blacksmith in 1837. Business was good at the sign of the "Red Wheel," on the corner of New Shallowford (Brookstown) and Main, and when Meinung's son, F. C., took over in 1884, it was the largest buggy works in Salem.

Courtesy of Historic Winston

The employees of F. & H. Fries' Flour and Grist Mill pause in the midst of their watermelon feast to have their picture taken about 1880. Standing from left to right are Daniel Barton, Lee Hanes, William H. Turner, John Spainhour, Andy Peddycord, driver Jim Spach, bookkeeper William Boyd, miller Curd Disher, and miller Samuel J. Shore. Crouching in front with a Rhode Island Red rooster on his knee is bookkeeper Frank Hege.

Courtesy of Bill East

Inspired by a visit by Thomas A. Edison, above, local people, along with Edison and Frank J. Sprague, an electric railway pioneer, formed on March 11, 1889 the Winston-Salem Street Railway Company, Incorporated. Sixteen months later, on July 14, 1890, the first electric streetcar rolled through the streets of Winston and Salem. The following year the company joined with the Winston Electric Light and Motive Power Company to form the Winston-Salem Railway and Electric Company. In the early days the line was pretty well confined to Fourth and Main Streets, extending to the Zinzendorf Hotel site on Fourth and to F. H. Fries Southside Mill in Waughtown. The line was later operated by the Fries Manufacturing and Power Company until, in 1913, it went public, being taken over by the Southern Public Utilities Company. The last streetcar in Winston-Salem was retired in December 1936, as the system fell victim to the rise of gasoline-powered buses and the private automobile.

Courtesy of Bill East

In 1822, the Salem Female Missionary Society was founded, and the following year they began a church for Salem's first black congregation. In 1827, a Sunday school was begun in which reading and writing, subjects forbidden by law to blacks in most of the South, were taught. A new building, upper left, was erected in 1862, and an addition made in 1890, whereupon the church was named St. Philip's. At the left, facing on Church at the intersection of Walnut is the Anna Johanna Vogler house (1827), occupied at the time of this picture by Harvey S. Crist. Below it on Church is the frame dwelling of T. F. Crist, whose daughter, Carrie, did photo retouching for Henry Lineback.

Photo by Henry A. Lineback

To promote use of their streetcar line, the Fries Manufacturing and Power Company built Nissen park at the southern terminus of the line in Waughtown. Opened in 1900, the park featured picnicking facilities, games, a miniature railroad, and the bowling alley shown here. Later there was a zoo, and, in 1916, motion pictures. At first the park was a great success, being especially favored for Sunday school picnics, but the growth of personal transportation made it easy for people to seek their pleasures wherever they chose, and the park folded in the 1920s.

Courtesy of Bill East

The car barn stood at the northwest corner of Church and Second Streets. Here the cars could be parked over open pits, giving the mechanics access to the undercarriage for maintenance and repairs. The site is now occupied by the new Federal Building.

Courtesy of the Frank Jones Collection

By 1890, Old Town (Trade) Street was the center of commerce for the town. Winston's fourth tobacco warehouse, the Piedmont, M. W. Norfleet and Company, stood at the left, fronting on Fourth. W. W. Wood and Company and T. L. Vaughn and Company, tobacco manufacturers, stood to the north, sandwiching John F. Griffith's grocery store. On the right, the tree stood in the yard of Mrs. F. J. Hardy's boarding house, established around 1880. Next came R. Turner's restaurant, and then, H. D. Poindexter's general merchandise store. Mr. Poindexter came from Yadkin County, and eventually, at the corner of Fifth and Spruce, he built a unique house, copied from that of J. G. Huff of East Bend. His descendants still own the house, endangered by plans for still another parking lot. Past Poindexter's, the awning marked the location of C. H. Loper's saloon, followed by A. B. Gorrell and Son's Farmers Warehouse. North of the warehouse were the dry goods concern of Dingelhoff and Bissinger and John A. Reid's grocery.

Courtesy of the Frank Jones Collection

In 1890, R. J. Reynolds took into partnership his brother, William Neal Reynolds, and a long time associate, Henry Roan. That same year he erected, on the original site, his first modern factory building. Shown above, building number 256, four stories and a basement fronting on Chestnut Street, was the finest factory building in town. Some time after 1900, a second building was erected where the houses stand on Second Street and connected to the first. Its elaborate facade, bearing the title "Building Number 256," has created confusion among modern observers. The first building is still in use, and except for minor alterations, its exterior is the same as it was in 1890.

Courtesy of Bill East

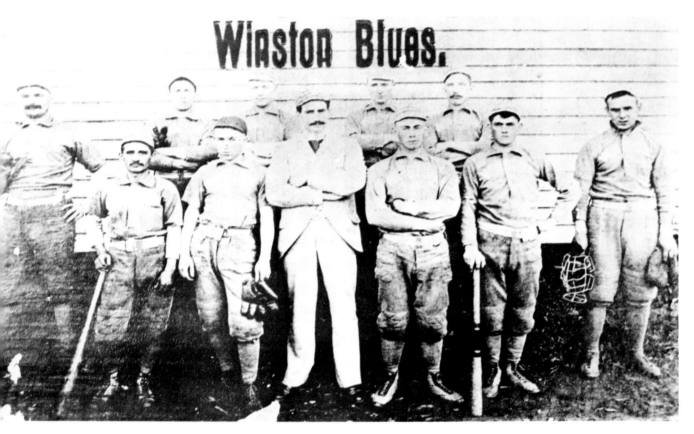

Baseball, a game of pastoral elegance, perfectly fit the pace of the times in the latter portion of the nineteenth century. Teams in the upper Piedmont area traveled by wagon to compete in weekend matches, the games becoming occasions for festive outings. Particularly hot rivalries might produce a rhubarb, with the visitors being chased out of town by the rabid fans of the home team. Over a period of five years in the 1890s, the famous Yadkin Red Strings lost only three games, two of them to the team from Winston. The Winston "Blues" of 1888 pose here for a team picture. They are, from left, first row: pitcher "Big" Liston, infielder "Shorty" Jones, outfielder Luther Bennett, manager Nathan Strawer, second baseman "Kid" Farrell, shortstop "Gigg" McGann, and catcher and substitute pitcher Monty Liston. Second row: pitcher C. M. Jones, captain "Ready" Sand, Andrew McGann and H. Kerner. "Kid" Farrell is still remembered by baseball oldtimers as a superb player who almost made it in the big leagues.

Courtesy of the Frank Jones Collection

In 1889, the West End Hotel and Land Company was formed, with the goal of constructing a series of resort hotels along the crest of the steep ridge on the western edge of Winston, there to take advantage of the cooling breezes and splendiferous views that dominated the summer months. By the spring of 1890, the first of these magnificent hostelries, the Zinzendorf, had been completed at Fourth and Glade, across from the present Grace Park. Streetcar lines had been extended to service the hotel, and hopes were high when the building opened for business, with rooms priced as high as three dollars.

A year-and-a-half later, on Thanksgiving Day, 1892, a small fire broke out in the laundry room. The fire companies from Salem and Winston raced each other down Fourth Street, the Winston engine being towed by a streetcar, for the honor of extinguishing the blaze. But trouble was encountered with the hydrants. There was insufficient water, so the hotel guests assisted in carrying out what furnishings could be salvaged, and the whole town sat back to watch. It was the event of the year.

The hotel burned to the ground, and with it went the hope of establishing Winston as a resort area. It was decided to keep commercial development, for the time, within the better protected central business district, and the West End was developed as a residential area, becoming in the later 1890s and early 1900s, Winston's finest.

Photo by Tom Hege

Early Winston was not known for its hotels, but the Hotel Jones was one of the better ones. It was located on Main Street where the second Zinzendorf Hotel would later stand, now the site of the plaza of the new Federal Building. Originally known as the Merchant's Hotel, it was operated in the 1880s by Pfohl and Stockton and later by W. R. Vickers, who came here from Durham. Around 1890, G. R. Quincy bought the property and operated it as the Hotel Quincy, before John L. Jones took over and gave his name to it. While under ownership of Pfhol and Stockton, the hotel had a reputation for the good food served there, and later, William Neal Reynolds, brother of R. J. Reynolds, would make his home there for a time. But in 1888 a critic stated bluntly that Winston's greatest shortcoming was its lack of a decent hotel.

Courtesy of Bill East

A two-horse open sleigh graces Main Street near the corner of Third in this 1890s winter scene.

Courtesy of the Wachovia Bank

From the bell tower of Home Church in the 1890s,
Salem spreads to the west. Shallowford Road
(Academy Street) runs from bottom to top, while in
the foreground are the roofs of the Inspector's House
(1810), now the Salem Book Store, and the Boy's
School (1794), now the Wachovia Museum. At left is
the Single Brothers' House (1769/1786). Near the
center is the frame home of W. E. Petersen, and
beyond, the Elm (Marshall) Street Moravian Chapel.
At the right on Main Street is the home of Thomas B.
Douthit, storekeeper, adjoining his wife's millinery
shop.

Courtesy of the Frank Jones Collection

These houses sat across the street from each other on Cherry between Fourth and Fifth. At the left is the home of William T. Brown, manager of the Southern Chemical Company. His opposite side neighbor was John W. Hanes, proprietor of the Shamrock Mills, later Hanes Hosiery.

Courtesy of Historic Winston

In Salem, Herbert A. Pfohl, manager of Fogle Brothers and president of the Church Lumber Company, built this two-and-one-half-story house on Bellews Creek Street. The building stood on the north side, between Church and Chestnut Streets.

Courtesy of Historic Winston

The ultimate in Victorian fantasy was this home, shared for nearly a decade by R. J. and W. N. Reynolds. When R. J. married Catherine Smith and brought her home to live, Mr. Will and his wife, Kate Bitting Reynolds, moved into M. N. Williamson's former home two buildings away. The Reynolds house stood at 666 West Fifth Street, now the site of the Public Library.

Courtesy of Historic Winston

W. Ernest Nissen, foreman of the C. F. Nissen Company, built this house near the wagon works. It stood at 2456 Waughtown Street.

Courtesy of Historic Winston

West Fourth Street looking east from Broad in the 1890s. At the left is the home of D. H. King, coal, ice, and bottling magnate, later occupied by J. E. Buxton. Across the street a part of the home of Mrs. Nannie Leak, widow of George Leak, tobacco manufacturer, is visible. By the turn of the century, Watt Martin, dealer in tobacco manufacturing supplies, was living there. Next is the home of realtor Cicero Tise. The large brick structure in the center is the second factory of the Walker Brothers, tobacco manufacturers. After Walker Brothers was swallowed up by Buck Duke's tobacco trust, the building was used as a shoe factory by the Jenkins Brothers, and later still was a warehouse for R. J. Reynolds Company. Around 1920, it was converted and operated as the Alexander Apartments and is today the home of the Inn Towne Motel. At the rear of the building can be seen the two-story frame structure that served as Walker Brothers' first factory and just above that is the four-story tobacco factory of Hodgin Brothers and Lunn on Marshall Street, later the first site for J. W. Hanes' Shamrock Mills. At upper right is Calvary Moravian Church, on Holly Avenue, and in the center background is the First Presbyterian Church, on Cherry. To the left along Fourth can be seen the steeple of the St. Paul's Episcopal Church on the corner of Pine (Marshall) and the belltower of Augsburg Lutheran Church on the corner of Spruce. Tom Hege climbed the tower of the old West End School to get his shot of peaceful coexistence among factories, churches, and fine residences. He wouldn't recognize the same view today.

Photo by Tom Hege

The Wachovia National Bank was established in June 1879 by Edward Belo, Wyatt F. Bowman, William A. Lemly, J. W. Hunter, James A. Gray, and others, with Mr. Bowman as president and Mr. Lemly, formerly with the First National Bank, as cashier. The first building stood near the north end of the present Hall of Justice on Main Street. By 1888, Wyatt Bowman was dead, succeeded by William Lemly, and the bank had moved into this ornately done building at the southwest corner of Third and Main. James A. Gray, the new cashier, mans his window at right, while his son-in-law, A. H. Galloway, gotten up in the fashion of the day, rests his arm on the counter at center. From left to right the others are thought to be Robert T. Gray, Emory S. Gray, and G. H. Brooks. While a customer, far left, prepares for a transaction, Lemly, center, and teller G. H. Brooks look on.

Courtesy of Mrs. A. H. Galloway

Just ten years after its founding, the Wachovia National Bank moved to the site, at the southwest corner of Third and Main, that would be home for its main offices for three-quarters of a century. The first of two buildings on that corner, where Robert Gray had built one of Winston's first stores, was completed in early 1889. Posing shortly after the opening are, left to right: George Brooks, teller, James A. Gray, cashier, and R. J. Reynolds. The building stood for barely two decades, being removed in 1910 to make way for Winston's first metal-frame skyscraper.

Courtesy of the Wachovia Bank

In 1872 C. A. Hege began making iron implements with a horse-turned lathe. Five years later he invented an improved circular saw-mill, and in 1882 he built the three-story factory at the center to house his expanding business. By the late 1880s, Salem Iron Works was producing wood-working machinery, steam engines, and other mechanical devices and had opened a branch plant in Apopka, Florida. Taken from the corner of First and Cherry in 1893 and looking to the southeast, this photograph shows, in the foreground, South Elm (Marshall) Street. The long low building behind the two-story frame house at right is the hosiery manufactory of A. G. Hough. The next street over is Salt (Liberty), and the double-chimneyed, three-story house at left is that of Mr. Hege.

Courtesy of Bill East

C. M. Thomas and D. H. King were Winston's pioneers in the coal and ice business. In the 1890s, Mr. Thomas built this trestle near the railroad yards. Hopper cars laden with coal could be driven onto the span, which provided bins into which they dumped their cargo, to be hauled away by wagons to supply the customers of the Thomas Coal Company.

Courtesy of Historic Winston

Immediately after the Civil War, W. L. and R. D. Brown began the manufacture of tobacco in Mocksville, the county seat of Davie County. In 1876 they moved their operation to Winston, setting up shop in a 50 by 150 foot, four story structure on the east side of Church Street, between Fourth and Fifth. They became one of the town's largest manufacturers, featuring such brands as "Old Oaken Bucket," "Stonewall," "Slap Jacks," and "Our Q." In 1895 they built the warehouse at the left, five and one-half stories with a mansard roof and gable windows. About five years before, W. F. Smith and Son had built the factory at the right, where they became one of Winston's first cigarette manufacturers. Both companies were swallowed up by the tobacco trust in the late 1890s, but the buildings were preserved, having for the last half-century been used by the Piedmont Leaf Tobacco Company, redriers and stemmers of leaf tobacco. The Smith factory, closely resembling R. J. Reynold's first building with its gabled roof and stepped gable facade, is the Twin City's only remaining example of pre-1890 tobacco architecture.

Photo by Fam Brownlee

C. J. Watkins graduated from the Pennsylvania College of Dental Surgery and served in the Civil War before setting up practice in Philadelphia in 1866. Eight years later he came back home, operating his office in his home on Main Street across from Voglers undertaking parlor. In 1886 he took W. J. Conrad as his partner in Watkins & Conrad, dentistry. Later Dr. Watkins entered the dental supply business with his son, J. Conrad Watkins, in the building at left. Dr. Watkins and his wife, Flora, are seen on the porch, surrounded by their children.

Courtesy of Bill East

The Democratic presidential ticket in 1892 was made up of Grover Cleveland and the first Adlai Stevenson. That summer, Stevenson came to Winston for a round of political drumbeating and speechmaking. Local Democrats got up the biggest show since the Chipmunk rally of 1852. When the doings were at their height, the organizers had their pictures taken on an old stagecoach in front of Charles Buford's house on Main Street, across from the present City Hall. Visible are Captain Charles Buford, Harry Samuels, Gustavus A. Follin, Will Brown, Eugene Hester, Thomas W. Huske, Frederick M. Roberts, Clement Manly, Captain John E. Gilmer, and Watt Martin. Captain Buford and Manly had, earlier that year, been delegates at the nominating convention in Chicago. In November, Cleveland and Stevenson won by a comfortable margin.

Courtesy of the Frank Jones Collection

The rear portion of the new municipal building housed the armory of the Forsyth Riflemen and the city market, the stalls of which were primarily occupied by meat sellers. At the right is number twelve East Fourth Street, the barber shop of R. D. Howlett.

Courtesy of the Frank Jones Collection

A part of the new municipal building, facing on Church Street, was known as the city market. This 1894 photo shows the stall of L. C. Crouch, who offered ice cream and milk shakes.

Courtesy of Bill East

In 1890, contributions by the town of Winston and private citizens of both communities were instrumental in persuading Colonel A. C. Davis to move his military academy, which had begun operations in La Grange in the 1880s, to the Twin City. At left, the cadets fall in for a dress parade along Liberty Street at the courthouse in 1894. Above is a view of the academy grounds with a baseball game in progress. Around 1900, the popularity of the school fell off and it was closed. In 1902, a fire destroyed the classroom buildings and one of the barracks. In 1909, the Methodist Church purchased the property for its Children's Home.

Courtesy of Bill East

In December 1887, the first hospital in Forsyth County opened its doors on Liberty Street, south of Third in the former home of Martin Grogan. The Twin City Hospital Association had been founded earlier that year at the home of Dr. Henry T. Bahnson by a group of civic-minded women headed by Aurelia Bowman Gray. The old Grogan home soon proved inadequate and the hospital closed in 1891.

Four years later it reopened in the above building on New Shallowford Street (Brookstown Avenue), where the Navy Reserve Center now stands. Conditions in the seventeen-bed hospital were primitive, with little equipment available, but a beginning had been made, and the building would serve until the construction of a modern, fire-proof facility in 1914.

Courtesy of Bill East

A view down Main Street from near Cascade in 1894. In the distance at center can be seen the tower of the new municipal building, flanked by church steeples and factory chimneys, the twin trademarks of the Twin City. Tom Hege, who took this picture, liked to enliven his views with people, which explains the presence of the boys in the foreground.

Photo by Tom Hege

During tobacco sale time, the farmers from the surrounding countryside would park their wagons in the streets while they eagerly watched over the auction process. Here the wagons line North Main Street between Fifth and Sixth near George S. Norfleet and Company's Star Warehouse. At right are the home and office of Dr. A. L. Mock.

Courtesy of Bill East

A cow grazes placidly in the field where First Street intersects the railroad yard in this mid-1890s photograph. Viewed from Belews Street to the north, R. J. Reynolds' building number 256 is at the left. The partially-obscured two-story building at left center is the old Richmond and Danville Railroad terminal, expanded and run down, but still standing today. Just to the right of the terminal is the wholesale grocery business of Edgar D. Vaughn and Company, and to the right of it, the warehouse of S. E. Allen's hardware business. Directly behind Allen's is the warehouse of W. B. Pollard and Company, leaf dealers. Farther to the right is the tobacco factory of Harvey and Rintels, and to the right of it, another tobacco factory, that of W. F. Smith and Sons (1890), still standing today under the ownership of the Piedmont Leaf Tobacco Company. Beyond it is the Brown Brothers Tobacco Company (1895), also a part of the Piedmont Leaf complex today.

Courtesy of the Frank Jones Collection

The Winston police force gathered for this group photograph in 1893. Standing, left to right: O. W. Hanner, Frank Martin, J. J. Cofer, W. M. Sugg, Henry Valentine, and John T. Thompson. Seated at the left is chief J. W. Bradford, who a few years before, while serving as the county jailor, was the executioner in the third of Forsyth County's four public hangings. Seated next to him is city tax collector and constable Jesse C. Bessent, who also served as first lieutenant in the Forsyth Riflemen. Mr. Martin was the city sanitary policeman, responsible for catching violaters of the town sanitation ordinances.

Courtesy of Winston-Salem Police Department

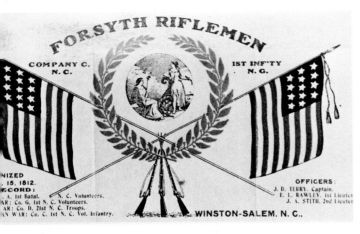

The Forsyth Riflemen was the first permanent military organization in Wachovia and the surrounding area, tracing its beginnings to Germantown during the War of 1812. In addition to their record as it appears here, they later served against Pancho Villa on the Mexican border and with the Thirtieth Infantry in World War I. At home they served as a backup for the police in case of civil disorder, as in 1895, when they were called out to break up a mob of two to three hundred blacks who had surrounded the jail to prevent a possible lynching.

Courtesy of Historic Winston

The Forsyth Riflemen, J. C. Bessent, Captain and J. D. Terry, First Lieutenant, turn out in full dress for an 1894 burial procession. To the beat of the drum they march south on Main Street toward Fourth, while business at Brown's Warehouse, right, goes on as usual. The two-story brick building at center is the Forsyth County jail, built in 1890 by Fogle Brothers, and equipped with an indoor gallows that was used only once, as most of the legal hangings in Forsyth county were done publicly at the County Poorhouse site on North Liberty Street. In the background above Fifth Street is the Star Warehouse.

Courtesy of Bill East

Cyrus B. Watson, attorney, came to Winston after the
Civil War. He was active in local government, serving
in various capacities, until in 1895, he decided to run
for governor on the Democratic ticket against
Republican Daniel L. Russell and Populist William A.
Guthrie. It was a bitter fight, and Watson introduced a
new weapon to North Carolina, the whistle-stop
campaign. In this picture he prepares for one such
jaunt, pausing only to pose with his friend and fellow
lawyer, Clement Manly, at right. Watson campaigned
hard, but overwhelmed by national issues, he lost to
the Republican Russell.

Courtesy of Bill East

On a hot summer day the watermelon vendors were a welcome sight for all. Here, several farmers prepare to set up shop in front of Wilson House, a boarding house operated by Mrs. Phoebe E. Wilson at 103 East Fourth Street across Church Street from the old City Market. The hickory trees in the yard provided a cool respite from the sun for the sellers of fruits and vegetables for a number of years. The site is now occupied by a Reynolds Tobacco Company factory.

Courtesy of the Frank Jones Collection

The mud flats below the iron bridge over Salem Creek were a popular spot for fishing and general goofing off in the 1890s. Here, in 1895, E. V. Patterson, left, and Tom Hege, at the camera, engage in the latter pursuit with their unidentified colleague, right. The man on the wagon is apparently a bemused bystander.

Photo by Frank C. Hege

Before battery-power took over the toy industry, balloons were a favorite plaything, and a balloon ascension was a major part of many public celebrations. Here the Odd Fellows prepare to send up a small balloon at their picnic in Nissen Park in 1894.

Courtesy of Bill East

Winston's First Baptist Church traces its beginnings to
a congregation of one man and four women who
began meeting in the courthouse in 1871. By the time
Henry Brown, a Civil War veteran and Wake Forest
College graduate, took over as pastor in 1877, they
had built a church on the north side of Second Street
between Church and Chestnut Streets. During his
forty years as minister, First Baptist became one of the
city's largest churches. Dr. Brown is seen here in the
sanctuary, decorated for the church's twenty-second
anniversary celebration.

Courtesy of the Frank Jones Collection

HE KILLED ELLEN.

DeGraff Makes a Confession on the Scaffold.

THE EXECUTION A SUCCESS.

Warned the People Not to Do as He Had Done.

DeGRAFF FACED DEATH BRAVELY.

THE DROP FELL AT 12:55—BROKE HIS NECK.

Death Instantaneous—Features Perfectly Natural After Death—The Condemned Man's Speech—Full Particulars of the Hanging—Visited at the Jail—Sad Scene—The Crime, Arrest and Trial—Over 6000 People Present.

Peter DeGraff is dead!

Sheriff McArthur sprung the trigger in the presence of at least 6,000 people at 12:52 and in an instant the life of the condemned man went out.

The neck was broken and death was instantaneous, but the heart's action continued for seven minutes as follows: 1st minute 48; 1st half of 2nd minute 62; last half of 2nd minute 28; 3rd minute 68; 4th minute 92; 5th minute 60; 6th minute 36; ceased in 7th minute.

ARRIVED AT THE SCAFFOLD.

It was just ten minutes past 12 o'clock when Sheriff McArthur and Jailer Ziglar ascended the scaffold with the condemned man. The rope was around his neck. DeGraff looked rather pale but appeared remarkably calm. He raised his hat and bowed to the crowd. He took a seat between the sheriff and Rev. H. A. Brown. He held a small bible with his hat in one hand.

DEATH WARRANT.

Sheriff McArthur arose to read the death warrant. He said; "Fellow citizens, this is indeed a very solemn occasion. Those who have

here, beware of bad women and whiskey.

The devil had such a great power over me that I thought I could almost walk with death without fear. He (the devil) said he would be with me.

I again say don't put your hands on cards, bad women and dice. Hear my dying words. I have washed my blood and hope those who have enmity against me will forgive me.

"May God bless you all is my prayer on this side of the bar of God."

ANOTHER PRAYER.

Rev. H. A. Brown offered another short prayer, after which Peter shook hands with his brothers, the preachers, sheriff, Chief-of-Police Bradford and Policeman Adams.

DeGraff gave his hat and small Bible to his youngest brother. After the black cap was placed over his head, it was lifted, at the request of the prisoner, who again shook hands with the sheriff.

AFTER DEATH.

When the cap was removed after the prisoner was taken down, the features of the dead man were found to be perfectly natural.

THE CROWD.

Six thousand people at least witnessed the execution. The road from town to the scene was lined with wagons, buggies and carts. Hundreds also traveled afoot. With many the event was no more than a circus. They were laughing and jesting all the time.

THE SCAFFOLD.

A rope was placed around the scaffold to keep the dense crowd off. The coffin, covered with a quilt, rested under the rear end of the scaffold.

A FALSE REPORT.

The report went the rounds on the

PETER DEGRAFF.

streets this morning to the effect that Peter DeGraff attempted to pump it

HIS OWN STORY!

A Sketch of Peter DeGraff's Eventful Career.

HE LED A RECKLESS LIFE,

Thinks That He Was Born at Elizabeth City, N. C.

MOVED TO WINSTON IN 1876.

TRIED AND ACQUITTED FOR CARRYING A PISTOL.

Worked in Virginia—How a Girl Fooled Him by Marrying Another Fellow—In Trouble With Another Girl—Returned to His Old Job—Engaged to Marry—She Loved; But He Didn't—The Ellen Smith Murder.

THE SENTINEL is permitted to give a sketch of Peter DeGraff's eventful life.

He told the story to Mr. M. M. Vickers, his night watchman, and speaks for itself.

WHERE HE WAS BORN.

I don't know just exactly where or when I was born, but guess I was born in Elizabeth City. N. C. about 1870. My parents told me we came to Winston in 1876 and came direct from Elizabeth City. I can't remember even living there. I visited there some years ago and found people who remembered my parents and remembered me as a very little boy when I left there.

LED A RECKLESS LIFE.

I don't know just how old I was when I began to attend Sunday School, but I was quite a small boy. I attended Sunday School first in Salem; had kind and good teachers; could call their names. They doubtless remember me; they gave me the best of advice. Later, I became secretary of a little Sunday School out in the country. If I had yielded to the precious influences that were tried to be brought to bear upon me, I would

Poor Ellen Smith, how was she found?
Shot through the heart, lieing dead on the ground.
The Kingston Trio made these lines familiar to an international audience in a single recording and on their "New Frontier" album in the early 1960s. Few who heard the song could know the grisly story behind the words of just another "folk hit" record. Many a local child had had his or her grandmother point out the spot where Ellen Smith was slain, and those lucky enough to have musical grandparents had heard the song.

Some time on the night of July 20-21, 1892, Peter DeGraff killed Ellen Smith in a lonely piece of woods behind the Zinzendorf Hotel, now the site of the Y.W.C.A. on Glade Street. It was, more or less, a lovers' spat, she having borne his illegitimate child. A night or so later, he returned to the scene of the crime, thus providing for his eventual undoing. On his last night among the living, he explained to a local reporter that someone had told him that if a murderer returns to the site of his misdeed and calls the name of the victim, the evil act would be undone. It was this Shakespearian touch that made the murder of Ellen Smith a local legend.

DeGraff eluded the immediate hue and cry, and it was nearly a year later before he was arrested by Sheriff McArthur near Rural Hall. Tried and convicted, DeGraff was sentenced to be hanged on Thursday, February 8, 1894. A crowd estimated at nearly six thousand gathered near the County Poorhouse on North Liberty Street, the current site of the offices of Piedmont Aviation, to witness the execution. Living eyewitnesses say that DeGraff's final speech, in which he confessed to the murder, contained a lesson worth taking to heart in its condemnation of "dice, cards, easy women, and hard liquor." DeGraff's father stated that he would rather see Peter hung than serve life in the penetentiary. He got his wish. A little before one o'clock in the afternoon, Peter DeGraff, Winston's most celebrated murderer, took the drop.

Courtesy of the Forsyth County Public Library

Sam Jones was a fire-breathing evangelist who stalked the Carolina-Virginia border in the 1890s. Here a typical audience is seen leaving Brown's Warehouse after a Jones performance in 1896. The evangelist was so popular that R. J. Reynolds brought out a plug brand called "Sam Jones Vest Chew." It was a period in which criticism was levelled at tobacco manufacturers for the impropriety of such brands as "Martha Washington," "Tom Jefferson," and "Stonewall Jackson." Reynolds came in for his share of the criticism, but P. H. Hanes probably reached the ultimate in exploitation with his brand designed for certain areas of the country: "Brigham Young."

Courtesy of the Frank Jones Collection

Calvary Moravian Church was constructed in 1888-89 on the Moravian Reservation at the corner of Holly and Poplar Streets. The congregation remained under the control of Home Church, with Bishop Edward Rondthaler as pastor, until 1893, when it achieved full independence. At the time of this turn-of-the-century photograph, the pastorate was held by the Reverend E. S. Crosland. In the early 1920s the present building was constructed, replacing Winston's first Moravian Church.

Courtesy of Historic Winston

The Centenary Methodist Episcopal Church replaced their 1850 edifice with this building, completed in 1887. Erected on the site of the original church, the structure was designed at a cost of thirty thousand dollars by a Richmond architect. The 135-foot bell tower was the tallest man-made object in the area, and the building served its congregation until the present Centenary Church was built on Fifth Street in 1929-31. The Reverend William R. Ware was pastor at the time of this 1901 photograph.

Courtesy of Historic Winston

The need for more churches increased with the expanding populace. By 1890, the original Methodist Episcopal Church has been supplemented by the founding of Burkhead M. E. Church (1886) on North Liberty Street. In that year, Winston's third M. E. church, Grace, was founded. At the time of this 1902 photograph, the church, located on Woodland Avenue at the corner of East Fourth Street, had as its pastor the Reverend Walter A. Willis.

Courtesy of Historic Winston

In the latter third of the nineteenth century, the smattering of Brethren living in what is now Buena Vista found themselves immersed by the swelling tide of Methodism. At an inconvenient distance from the Moravian churches in Salem and Bethabara, they began holding services under a brush arbor in 1884. Five years later, they built a sanctuary and gave the name of their rustic beginnings to the Wachovia Arbor Moravian Church and to Arbor Road. By 1893 the congregation had outgrown the tiny church and the present structure, shown here, was erected. Defying the trend to "bigger is better," Wachovia Arbor Church, under the direction of former lay minister J. C. Crook, survives, with approximately fifty communicants, to this day.

Courtesy of Historic Winston

The Reverend William A. Lutz founded Augsburg Lutheran's congregation in 1891. The following year, this brick and stone structure, built after a design by a Swedish architect, was begun on Fourth Street at the corner of Spruce. Completed in 1895, the church at the time of this 1902 photograph had as its pastor the Reverend C. A. Ritchie. The present Augsburg Church building replaced Winston's first Lutheran church in 1928.

Courtesy of Historic Winston

Thought to be the oldest dwelling still standing in Buena Vista, this house was built by J. H. Poole in 1882 on the Brookstown (Robin Hood) Road, near the present intersection with Coliseum Drive. Mr. Poole and his family arrived from Raleigh in late 1881 and occupied the old plank road toll house near the intersection of Kent and Reynolda Roads while the land was purchased and the building erected with the help of neighbors at an old fashioned "house raising." The house served, for many years, as the center of operations for a large farm, part of which occupied the site of the present College Village Apartments, and is still in the hands of descendants of the original builder.

Courtesy of Historic Winston

In 1816, Karsten Petersen of Denmark took over the old Single Brothers' abbatoir and converted it into a cabinetmaking shop. When this picture was taken eighty years later, his sons William and James E. were still operating the business at the same site on Shallowford (Academy) Street, below the Brothers' House. Within a few years they had retired, and the only third generation son trained in woodworking, Nathaniel V. Petersen, was working for Fogle Brothers.

Courtesy of Bill East

C. A. Winkler poses in front of his bakery on Main Street, just above Academy, in the 1890s. The building was erected in 1800 and was used as a bakery into the 1920s. Old Salem, Incorporated, has restored the shop, and visitors may watch bread and pastries being baked in the ancient oven. The building at the right housed the music hall and Salem's first museum. To the left of the bakery is the Butner house (1829) and shop (1825). The next building visible is the Vorsteher's house (1797), which once housed the Wachovia Land Office and is now the Moravian Church Archives, Southern Province.

Courtesy of the Frank Jones Collection

Main Street in Salem, looking south from near Bank Street. At the right is the Schroeter house and tailor shop, built in 1805. Next to it, the three-story frame building housed Thomas B. Douthit's granite works. The old Miksch tobacco shop (1771) next door served as living quarters for the Douthit family, and below it, Mrs. Julia G. Douthit operated her millinery establishment. B. F. Crosland's old store, on the site of the Triebel House (1775), stood on the corner across from the Moravian Widows Home, formerly the Single Brothers' House (1769/1786).

Courtesy of the Frank Jones Collection

John Phillip Nissen began, in 1834, the manufacture of wagons about two miles southeast of Salem in what is now Waughtown. His wagons went west with the forty-niners and later served to bring tobacco from the farms to the sales warehouses in Winston. At his death in 1874, Nissen had sold more than five thousand wagons. The business was taken over by his sons, George E. and William M. Nissen, and operated by them on into the twentieth century. Their works, above, was located on Waughtown Street. In the 1870s, J. I. Nissen began his own wagon works nearby. At the time of the photo, below, in the 1890s, the business had passed to the hands of his son, Christian F. Nissen. The works was located on Waughtown Street, a block past the intersection with Clover.

Courtesy of the Frank Jones Collection

A "NISSEN" CARRYING TWENTY TIMES ITS OWN WEIGHT

A "NISSEN WAGON" of 8,000 pounds rated capacity, weighing only 1,000 pounds, carrying a mammoth Rock Crushe weighing 20,000 pounds, which is twenty times the weight of the Wagon, and two and one-half times its rated capacity. You wil often find "NISSEN WAGONS" in daily use carrying nearly twice their rated capacity, day in and day out.

"Nissen Wagons" DO Give Service

This advertisement for Nissen Wagons was run around the turn of the century.

Courtesy of Bill East

F. & H. Fries was a company that believed in diversification. Here, around 1900, we see their ice plant on South Marshall Street at Shallowford (Brookstown). The ice was made by compressors powered by coal-fired steam engines. The wooden structure at the left is a cooling tower used to recycle the water for the boilers. Most of the buildings pictured have now been leveled.

Courtesy of the Frank Jones Collection

F. & H. Fries employees take time out for a photograph and a little horseplay in 1894.

Courtesy of the Frank Jones Collection

The Fries cotton manufactories got as much usage as possible from the streetcars. Here two open cars haul bales of cotton between the plants in Salem and the Southside.

Courtesy of Historic Winston

In the early 1890s, George T. Brown, a former tobacco worker, and Robert L. Williamson, late an employee of T. L. Vaughn and Company, combined to form the Brown and Williamson Tobacco Company. They purchased the old schoolhouse lot at the corner of First and Liberty and put up their "Model" tobacco works. By the early 1900s, in defiance of Buck Duke's tobacco trust, they were the largest independent flatplug tobacco manufacturers in the United States, putting out such brands as "Kite," "Sweet and Juicy," "Blood Hound," and "Maginty Twist." By then the company had begun to center its operations in Louisville, Kentucky, where its main offices are now located. The buildings on Liberty Street were torn down for a parking lot, although artifacts of the tobacco complex are still visible in the form of some foundations and a lone brick tower near the south end of the lot.

Courtesy of Historic Winston

R. B. Crawford came to Winston in 1883 and began a business in hardware at the corner of Fourth and Liberty. He specialized in grain machinery, with his top lines being the Deering Twine Binder and the Deering and Meadow King Mowers. The business was a success, and in 1893, Mr. Crawford erected the Crawford Building, pictured here, on Fourth Street near Liberty. Note the unusual lion statue used as a street sign. The building, next to the Pepper Building, is one of the oldest still standing in the central business district.

Courtesy of Historic Winston

William Barrett Taylor, posing here on his horse Prince in front of his home at Fourth and Brookstown, was the individualist of Winston's tobacco manufacturers. Beginning in 1883, "Old Man Bill" soon took into partnership his brother, Jaquelin P. Taylor, forming the Taylor Brothers Company, at First and Depot (Patterson) Streets. Known as an eccentric and labeled a "socialist," he was a man of deep religious conviction, requiring that his workers begin each day at the plant with hymns and prayers. Quick of wit and sharp of tongue, he resisted Buck Duke's trust and all later efforts at absorption of his company, and his brands, "Bull of the Woods," "Black Maria," "Red Coon," and "Peach and Honey," were among the best of their time. He died in 1933, leaving a host of "Old Man Bill" stories and a legacy of independence to his sons. The company, one of the last of the independents, was finally sold to the American Snuff Company in 1952. Mr. Taylor's house still stands on Fourth Street next to Grace Park.

Courtesy of Historic Winston

The interior of the Wachovia Loan and Trust Company at 220 Main Street in Winston reveals standard banking decor in the latter part of the nineteenth century. The building was modern in every respect, with electric lights and a fireproof vault. Note especially the ornate grillwork and the spittoons.

Courtesy of Historic Winston

W. H. Hughes, known as "Winston's Fashionable Barber," opened his shop in 1894 at 107 West Fourth Street, near the corner of Liberty. Note the ceiling fan and the chair for shoeshines in the foreground.

Courtesy of Historic Winston

Winston's ladder truck and crew pose in front of the Jones Hotel on Main Street around the turn of the century. Holding the nozzle at the rear is Tom Keith, while perched on the driver's seat with the ubiquitous dog is Watt Knight. Standing at left is Bob Shelton and next to him is Winston's first paid fireman, John H. Holmes. No fire department picture is complete without its gathering of boys. Red Powell, under the horse's head, and his chums provide that final touch.

Courtesy of the Frank Jones Collection

The manufacture of chewing and pipe tobacco and cigarettes is a well-known fact of life in the Twin City. A lesser known industry is evidenced in this 1890s photograph by the advertisement for "Fair Sex" and "Havatra" five cent cigars. These brands were manufactured by A. R. Bennett and Company in their factory at 612-614 West Four-and-One-Half Street. Bennett's partner, John H. Leonard, had operated a small cigar manufactory since the 1880s, and others, such as druggist V. O. Thompson, had begun even earlier, but the local cigar industry never amounted to much, as the big money flowed into the easier to make plug and smoking brands. The man examining the animal pelt provides stark contrast to the advertisement, giving evidence that, despite twenty years of vigorous industrial development, the town of Winston still bore the marks of its primitive beginnings.

Courtesy of the Frank Jones Collection

110

Tom Keith, Bob Shelton, and John Holmes stuck around for the portrait of Winston's steam pumper. Perched on the hose is Jule Stith and in the driver's seat is Tom Graham.

Courtesy of the Frank Jones Collection

Tobacco wagons flocking to Brown's Warehouse clog Main Street in this turn-of-the-century view, looking north from Fourth. Behind the wagon at right is the shop of J. A. Gentry, watchmaker. Between there and the warehouse, Alexander Pace and Emmett Hawkins, both blacks, operated restaurants, next to F. H. Farabee's restaurant and grocery. Beyond the warehouse the corner of the Forsyth County jail can be seen. The row of buildings at left houses Brown, Rogers and Company's warehouse, the offices of J. A. and C. E. Bennett, contractors and suppliers of granite and marble, and the dry goods store of Marler and Dalton. Above the Marler and Dalton store was the office of H. H. Hall, the town's first black doctor.

Courtesy of Bill East

Salem's "Rough and Ready" fire company holds a drill in front of the original girls' boarding school building around 1890. In 1888, the *Union Republican* reported that the company's Button steam pumper could throw water over the tower of Centenary Methodist Episcopal Church, a vertical distance of 135 feet. The boarding school structure was built in 1805. Beyond it can be seen the academy's Main Hall (1854) and Home Church (1800). In the foreground is the Single Sisters' House (1786/1821).

Courtesy of Old Salem, Inc.

Hands of tobacco are laid out in neat piles awaiting the buyers and the chant of the auctioneer. This interior view of a sales warehouse was taken in the late 1890s. The signs hanging from the rafters advertise P. H. Hanes' chewing brands.

Courtesy of the Frank Jones Collection

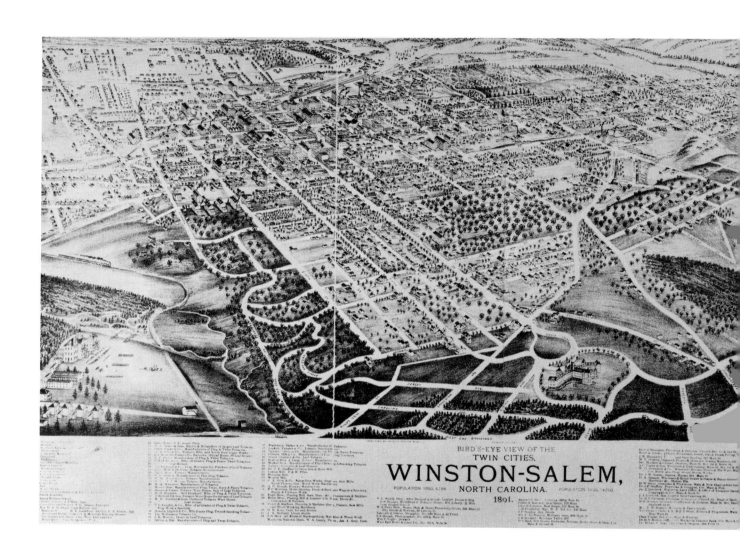

BIRD'S-EYE VIEW OF THE
TWIN CITIES,
WINSTON-SALEM,
NORTH CAROLINA.
1891.

A rare turn-of-the-century view, looking southeast past the intersection of Liberty and Seventh Streets, shows the steady march northward of industry along the Main, Church, Chestnut, and Depot arteries. At left is the Tise Manufacturing Company, makers of well fixtures and tobacco machinery. Near the center is an R. J. Reynolds warehouse and behind it, the spinning plant of P. H. Hanes. In the center, on the east side of Liberty, is the home of Mrs. M. A. Masten, while at right are the homes of C. B. Naylor and A. L. Stevenson.

Courtesy of Historic Winston

John A. Bennett began, in the 1880s, the quarrying of granite for monuments, headstones, and other uses. By 1900, he had taken in Charles E. Bennett as his partner in the Winston-Salem Granite Works. Their quarry, located six miles southwest of the town, is shown here. Their offices were located at 430 Main Street, opposite Brown's Warehouse, and their cutting shed at the corner of Bank and Salt Streets in Salem.

Courtesy of Historic Winston

Hege Brothers, Allie C. and Oscar F. Hege, proprietors, opened their store on Fourth Street above Liberty in the late 1890s. They specialized in bicycles, sporting goods, hardware, and photo supplies, advertising, in the camera line, besides George Eastman's Kodaks, such collectors' items as Premo, Pocco, Alvista, Panoramic, and Korona. Later, the company moved to Main Street, opposite the courthouse. Here, Oscar poses beside one of his cameras at 303 Main Street, Winston.

Courtesy of the Frank Jones Collection

Born in Prussia, Joseph Jacobs came to America in 1869. Seven years later he opened a clothing store on Main Street in Winston, becoming, probably, Winston's first Jewish businessman. By 1897 he had erected the Jacobs' Block along the east side of Main Street, which housed, besides his own store, a boot and shoe shop and various offices. Above his store was Jacobs' Hall, where the first Hebrew congregation held its services. Mr. Jacobs served several terms on the city board of commissioners and was for a time a director of the People's National Bank. The site of his building is now occupied by the parking lot at the corner of Main and Third Streets.

Courtesy of Historic Winston

David H. Browder, around the turn of the century, opened a book store on the O'Hanlon corner. The shop was L-shaped, with entrances at 404 Liberty Street and 105 West Fourth. By 1902, he was in partnership with William A. Watkins, a name that continues to this day in local bookselling. The store carried many of the same items as a modern day one, but on the second floor had a complete line of toys, pictures, and fancy goods.

Courtesy of Historic Winston

In the late 1890s, James E. Ziglar, a farmer, opened this livery stable on Liberty Street in the community known as Fairview. He and his wife, Martha, lived in the rear portion of the building.

Courtesy of Historic Winston

The Twin City Golf Club, which had its beginnings in a cow pasture near the intersection of Twelfth and Liberty Streets in 1897, was the first such association in North Carolina. Within a year, under the tutelage of John and David Blair, it was a going concern, with holes named after Bret Harte's western locales. The members chose the tee of the 250-yard Poker Flat hole for their first group picture. Left to right they are David Blair, Lila Young Alexander, Charles Tomlinson, W. S. Snipes, Daisy Vaughn Gilmer, Lou Gorrell Farris, Eleanor "Birdie" Follin, George Gibbs, Mamie Gray Galloway, A. H. "Eck" Galloway, Edna Maslin, Adelaide Fries, Alfred Belo, Jr., Marion Follin, Lottie Tomlinson Morrison, Phil Lybrook, John Blair, and Will Blair. The little girl seen as a blur in front of Will Blair is Margaret Blair McCuiston. Unfortunately, the caddies seated in front and the boy behind the Poker Flat sign are unidentified. The club flourished until the founding of the Forsyth County Club in 1910 drained off most of its members.

Courtesy of Terrell Young

At the turn of the century, social activities tended to be highly organized. Clubs were popular with civic leaders, male and female, and the younger set was quick to follow its elders. The "L-Cat" Club, its title a polite form for "Hell-Cat," was a good example, founded by the young men of prominent families for purely social purposes. Here they pose, with what might be called their "ladies' auxiliary," on the lawn of the F. P. Miller home, on Summit Street at the corner of Fifth. Left to right, they are, first row (on ground): Christine Crawford Walker, Fletcher Bailey, Henry Shelton, Frank Miller. Second row: Edmund Patterson, Caro Buxton Edwards, Daisy Hanes Lassiter, Sadie Hanes Connor, Ida Farish Jenkins, May Barber Follin, Bessie Dixon, Ida Miller Galloway. Back row: Lillie Brown, Charles G. Hill, Rob Follin, Cameron Buxton, Frank Vaughn, Clint Miller, and an unidentified woman. The life-span of the "L-Cat" club is not recorded, but Mr. Miller's magnificent home was demolished in 1959 by St. Paul's Episcopal Church. The site is now a parking lot.

Courtesy of Bill East

In conjunction with the tobacco fair of 1898, a tournament recalling the age of chivalry was held. The young men of Winston took knightly names and competed at spearing rings for the right to crown the queen of the carnival. The Knight of the White Knight, better known as Word Wood, came away with seven rings and placed the crown upon the head of the Queen of Love and Beauty, Miss Mamie Gray, seen here on her magnificent flower-bedecked float. Such were the pleasures of the day in old Winston town.

Courtesy of Mrs. A. H. Galloway

Before the coming of the automobile, many young couples in the Twin City relied upon streetcars for transportation to social events. But when the need to break away came upon them, they had solutions to the problems of private transit. Here we see Caro Buxton and Frank Rogers perched on the ultimate in social transit, the bicycle built for two, while at right, Cam Buxton and Sadie Hanes model the more conventional single-seaters. For longer distances, they took to the horse and buggy, below. On the bikes at rear of the buggy are Clint Miller and Frank Rogers, while R. Walton Nading and Robert W. Gorrell flank the young lady, thought to be Anna D. Harvey. The buildings behind them are occupied by Hine and Shipley, Harness, Saddles & Co., and Huntley, Hill and Stockton, furniture dealers. Like the horse and buggy, both firms are only memories.

Courtesy of the Frank Jones Collection

Winston and Salem got electric power in the 1880s, but production costs were high due to the use of gas generators. Consequently, in the summer of 1897, the Fries Manufacturing and Power Company began construction of a hydroelectric power plant. They chose a site, distinguished by a natural outcropping of rock, on the Yadkin River near Clemmons. The place had previously been the site of Douthit's mill, to the left of the powerhouse, but was known as Idol's, for the man who had operated a ferry there. Construction was under the direction of Charles A. Reynolds, and in the spring of 1898 the five-hundred-foot long, ten-foot-high dam was completed. At noon on April 18 of that year, little Marguerite Fries threw the switch, and the first long distance transmission hydroelectric power system in the South went into operation. The power was fed to a triangular building housing the transformers at Marshall and Shallowford (Brookstown) Streets in Salem. In 1914, the original turbines and generators were replaced by vertical models manufactured by the Allis-Chalmers Company. The dam and powerhouse, almost unchanged externally, are still in use, and the transformer building, although no longer serving its original purpose, remains intact.

Courtesy of Bill East

From the beginning, Pilot Mountain had a mystical allure for residents of the surrounding area. Here a party of Twin Citians use ladders for scaling the granite knob on a turn-of-the-century outing.

Courtesy of the Frank Jones Collection

The Winston mayor and board of aldermen in 1905. Top, left to right: Joseph O. White, Fourth Ward, a manufacturer of wagons and other vehicles; W. B. Pollard, First Ward; J. R. Cummings, Fourth Ward, operator of a grocery at Liberty and Depot (Patterson); W. N. Reynolds, First Ward, representing the Reynolds Tobacco Company; A. J. Gales, Third Ward, a contractor and captain of Fire Company Number One. Middle, left to right: William G. Cranford, Second Ward, of the blacksmith firm Spach and Cranford; Erastus R. Messick, Second Ward, a wholesale grocer; Mayor John F. Griffith, president of the Piedmont Savings Bank and a native of Davie County; Rufus I. Dalton, Fifth Ward, chairman of the finance committee and president of the Winston Furniture Company; Joseph Jacobs, a Main Street clothing merchant. Bottom, left to right: William E. Franklin, First Ward, a fire insurance broker; J. B. Vaughn, Third Ward, president of J. B. Vaughn and Company, wholesale grocers; C. M. Thomas, Second Ward, manager and bookkeeper for D. H. King's ice and coal business and Eugene W. Vaughn, Fifth Ward, of Ogburn, Hill and Company.

Courtesy of Historic Winston

During the 1890s and the early part of the first decade of the twentieth century, major changes were made on Trade Street. Rosenbacher and Brother, Joseph and Sigmund, had purchased Mrs. Hardy's boarding house and erected a building, moving their business from Third Street to the new site. On the left, the Piedmont Warehouse was gone, and construction was underway on the Masonic Temple, to be completed in 1906. Forsyth Hardware Company replaced W. W. Wood's tobacco factory. The only businesses remaining intact were Gorrell's Farmer's Warehouse and H. D. Poindexter's Store. Between them, Holbrook and Winfree had established a restaurant and saloon, the Criterion, advertising fish, oysters, and game in season, as well as foreign and domestic liquors, wines, and ales.

Courtesy of Bill East

In 1899 the post offices of Winston and Salem were consolidated. The first Winston-Salem post office, shown here, was located at the southeast corner of Main and Third Streets in the old Pfohl and Stockton store of 1876. Upstairs were the law offices of Eugene E. Gray, who also sold insurance, and the law firm of Adolphus E. Eller and Henry P. Starbuck, who would later become a Superior Court judge. Eller also was involved in insurance, having as his partner in that venture R. W. Nading.

Courtesy of the Wachovia Bank

As the commercial center of Winston became more congested, the tobacco warehouses, with their need for parking space for many wagons, were gradually pushed to the north. By 1910, M. W. Norfleet and Company's Piedmont Warehouse, at left, had moved up a block and across the street on Trade, bringing in its wake the stores that specialized in serving the visiting farmers. From the right, on the opposite side of the street, are the general merchandise concerns of Bennett and Tesh Company, J. Emra Cox, and B. A. Miller and Company.

Courtesy of Historic Winston

By 1910, automobiles were not unknown on Winston's streets. Two early autos pass on Liberty Street, while a streetcar crosses the intersection with Fourth, heading south on Liberty. At left, the awning shades the entrance to McDowell and Rogers' Clothing Store. Just north of E. W. O'Hanlon's office building and drug store, the Meyers-Westbrook dry goods emporium has replaced D. D. Schouler's Racket Store. Next came two of Winston's first department stores, The Leader and A. Daye and Company. Farther along stood the Elite Bowling Alley. Along Fourth, from Liberty, are J. A. Neely's shoe shop, P. A. (son of founder V. O.) Thompson's drug store and the barber shop of Russ and Spry. Near the center can be seen the cupola of the new Federal Building on Fifth Street.

Courtesy of Bill East

In the early 1890s, William A. Jones began selling drugs in conjunction with Dr. J. W. Jones' medical office on Main Street. By the turn of the century he had moved his expanding business to 110½ East Fourth Street, across from the Municipal Building. Here he poses for a 1907 photograph in his electric fan and soda fountain equipped establishment.

Courtesy of the Frank Jones Collection

Fourth Street, looking east from atop the new Y.M.C.A. building on the corner of Cherry around 1910. At lower left can be seen part of the lawn of Wyatt Bowman's old home. The Masonic Temple (1906), stands at the corner of Trade and across from it is Rosenbacher Brothers building, later Efird's department store. At the corner of Liberty is the O'Hanlon Drug Company, with Winston's first Municipal Building (1892) in the background.

Courtesy of Historic Winston

With the movement of Winston's prosperous businessmen into the West End, large mansions were built along Fourth, Fifth, Summit, and Glade Streets. In the early part of the century, J. C. Tise built this one at 952 West Fourth Street, and with its spacious porches and imposing columns it is typical of the genre. Today it is occupied by the Woman's Club.

Courtesy of the Frank Jones Collection

Looking west down Fourth toward Liberty about 1910. The soldier atop the Confederate monument, erected in 1905, watched over the Phoenix Hotel, constructed in 1893 after the first Zinzendorf Hotel burned. The hotel's cafe and main entrance are at left, the rest of its first floor being occupied by shops such as W. T. Vogler and Son, Jewelers, on the corner. Across the street is the O'Hanlon Drug Company. Going west on Fourth, the upper-story awnings mark the Carolina Hotel. The five-story building near the center is the Masonic Temple at the corner of Trade and in the distance is the bell tower of the Augsburg Lutheran Church. By the time of the depression, all the buildings over two stories in height would be gone and the sign on the courthouse lawn would have less grass to warn people off of.

Courtesy of the Frank Jones Collection

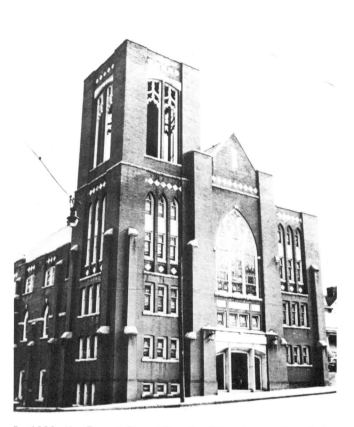

Fourth St., and Masonic Temple, Winston-Salem, N.

In 1889, the Broad Street Baptist Church was founded to serve the growing population of the West End. It was the third Baptist Church in Winston. In 1909, the Broad Street congregation erected this building on Fourth at Spring Street and gave it the name of Brown Memorial in honor of the late Reverend Henry A. Brown. It served the congregation for twenty-six years until their absorption by First Baptist in 1935. Eight years later, the Greek Orthodox congregation, founded in 1926, took over the building and used it until the mid-1960s. The structure was razed shortly thereafter.

Courtesy of Bill East

The Masonic Temple was constructed at the corner of Fourth and Trade in 1906, and torn down twenty years later for no good reason. The remains of its granite columns now reside in the back yard of a home in Kernersville.

Courtesy of Historic Winston

The West End Methodist Church, completed in 1913 at the corner of Fourth and Brookstown, capped Winston's first extravagant era of church building. If its seventy thousand dollar-plus cost was not enough to boggle the mind, its design, multiturreted Romanesque, certainly was. The wealthy citizens of the West End wanted nothing less than the best, and it would be more than a decade before any local church could approach the cost and flamboyance of their edifice. The church burned in the middle of the century.

Courtesy of the Frank Jones Collection

The East Salem Chapel, on Belews Street near Greenwood, was one of the first satellites founded by Home Church. The building is shown here in 1914. Standing near the front door are, left to right, George A. Boozer, Henry E. Fries, and Ada Parrish. The pastor was the Reverend John F. McCuiston.

Courtesy of the Frank Jones Collection

By the turn of the century, most of the prime lots at the crest of the ridge in West End were taken, and development began to spill over to the west. Between then and the beginning of the First World War these houses were constructed on the graceful, plunging curve where Glade Street runs down toward West End Boulevard. From left to right, they were the homes of Mrs. Mary C. Thompson (circa 1915), Cary L. Carroll (circa 1908), and Dr. Charles S. Lawrence (circa 1912), whose hospital is now the Rescue Mission. The stairs at left led to the home of Powell Gilmer of Gilmer Brothers Company.

Courtesy of the Frank Jones Collection

In 1902, Pleasant Henderson Hanes returned to the industrial scene. At the corner of Church and Sixth he built this textile complex, soon to become the world's largest manufacturer of men's underwear. The main building is an excellent example of turn-of-the-century industrial construction with its mansard roof and gabled dormer windows. At least two specimens survive in Forsyth County, the Inn Towne Motel (Walker Brothers Tobacco factory) on Fourth Street in Winston-Salem and the old Harmon and Reed Feed Mill in Kernersville.

Courtesy of the Hanes Corporation

By 1910, P. H. Hanes had expanded as far as he could in downtown Winston. That year he began construction on the road to Clemmons of a new spinning plant and the mill village that would bear his name. When completed, the village would have its own church, school, and volunteer fire department. This photograph shows a cluster of new dwellings, with the company store at left.

Courtesy of the Hanes Corporation

The Winston Industrial Insurance association was founded in 1906 by a group of black businessmen with the purpose of consolidating the baffling array of insurance policies available to members of the black community. Up until that time, policies had been offered by individuals or small partnerships, many of questionable financial stability, and fly-by-night operators were not unknown. Under its first slate of officers, J. S. Fitts, president; Dr. J. W. Jones, treasurer; R. W. Brown, secretary; and J. A. Blume, general manager, the company flourished, and in 1915 was renamed the Winston Mutual Life Insurance Company. By the time this photograph was taken in the 1940s, the home office and agency forces could boast a staff of more than fifty employees. The firm has recently occupied its fine new office building at 1225 East Fifth Street and is currently celebrating its seventieth anniversary.

Courtesy of Mrs. Myrtle Hairston Stepp

When the new Zinzendorf Hotel opened in 1906, it boasted one of the finest saloons in the state. For two years it would rival Holbrook and Winfree's famous "Critereon" in volume of business. It was the era of elegant mustaches, chewing tobacco, and ragtime music, and the Zinzendorf provided a respectable place for those in the know to prop a foot on the brass rail, down some cold suds or a shot of Casper or Shore or Williams' best, and talk baseball and politics. In 1908, the state legislature put a stop to the supply and the saloon closed for good.

Courtesy of the Frank Jones Collection

As Winston grew into a full-fledged industrial center, the need for commercial haulers increased. Early in the second decade of the twentieth century, Paul M. McGraw established McGraw Transfer and Storage at 120 East Third Street. Within three years Adam W. Lentz had joined him in the firm of McGraw and Lentz. By 1918 Lentz had bought out McGraw's interest in the business. McGraw opened the Third Street Bowling Alley and American Union Lunch at 11 and 13 East Third, and Lentz went on to build up the company now known as Lentz Transfer and Storage Company. The firm now occupies the old Arista-Salem Cotton Mill Complex on Brookstown Avenue.

Courtesy of the Frank Jones Collection

The automobile brought about a revolution in travel, but in the early days, doctors were among the few who could justify the expense. Dr. and Mrs. Henry H. Kapp show off their brand new Buick landaulet in July 1909. Mrs. Laura A. Cox, their nurse, holds their two sons, Henry Herman and Hege, who later followed his father into the medical profession.

Courtesy of Historic Winston

Frank Eddleman of Yadkin County opened, in the 1890s, a saloon at the northwest corner of Fifth and Church Streets. In 1905 he took in Crawford K. Todd as his partner. By the time of statewide prohibition in 1908, Eddleman had gone into partnership with Pleasant A. Davis in a fancier saloon at 118 East Third Street, while Todd remained at the old location with a new partner, L. J. Shore. Next door stood the barber shop of Pinckney Smith, while at center left, a portion of Ella Claiborne's restaurant and home is visible. On Main Street, next to the Star Warehouse, was the home of F. Leonard Ziglar. On the opposite side of Main, left to right, are the houses of J. G. Flynt, of J. G. Flynt and Company, tobacco manufacturers, and Mrs. Carrie Rosenbacher, widow of Sigmund, the founder of Rosenbacher and Brother.

Courtesy of Historic Winston

The first scheduled train of the Winston-Salem Southbound Railroad chugs onto the trestle over Salem Creek. The time is 2:50 p.m., November 24, 1910. The Southbound was a homegrown line and operates today as one of the few independents to survive the cataclysmic upheavals in the railroad industry that began after World War II.

Courtesy of the Frank Jones Collection

The Winston-Salem Southbound Railroad, founded by the vision of the Fries family and financed by local subscription, was begun in 1905. At top left workmen are building one of the viaducts over a small stream south of town, while at center other workmen erect the trestle across Salem Creek. In 1910, the first train, bottom, left the station and moved out onto the trestle. The little girl in the cab is Mary Louise Collier. The railroad eventually reached Wadesboro, eighty miles distant. It is one of the few truly independent lines still operating today.

Courtesy of Bill East

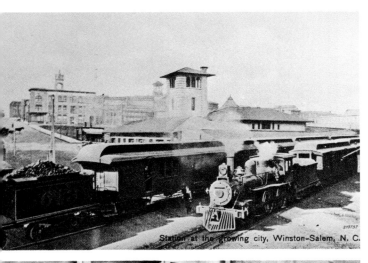

Station at the growing city, Winston-Salem, N. C.

With the opening of the Southbound, Winston's need for a central passenger terminal to service all lines increased. Accordingly, in 1916, the Union Railroad Station opened at the corner of Third and Chestnut Streets. It would serve the railroads and the citizens of Winston-Salem for ten years until a much larger and more elaborate structure on Claremont Avenue replaced it in 1926. The towers in the background are those of the second Forsyth County courthouse, left, and the first City Hall, center.

Courtesy of Historic Winston

On April 7, 1910, the founders of the one-day-old Huntley-Hill-Stockton Company posed proudly in front of their building at the corner of Fifth and Trade. The driver of their shiny new chain-drive truck is unidentified, but the others are, left to right, B.F. Huntley, M. D. Stockton, J. Frank Morris and, almost out of the picture, F. Jake Krouse. Not being the kind of men to miss a business opportunity, they soon were operating the city's first ambulance. The attendants are Henry L. Hanes, left, and S. F. Morris.

Courtesy of the Frank Jones Collection

A. C. Vogler began, around 1858, the manufacture of coffins and furniture in his shop on Main Street between Belews Creek and North (First) Street. After being taken into the business in 1887, his son, Frank H. Vogler, obtained a degree from the Oriental School of Embalmers, and the Twin Cities got their first modern undertaking establishment. Here we see the Vogler establishment shortly before the First World War. Vogler Service, now with two branch offices, is the city's oldest business in continuous operation at the same site.

Courtesy of Bill East

Having emerged intact from the tobacco trust, R. J. Reynolds, in 1913, put out his first line of cigarettes. Four brands, Reyno, Osman, Red Kamel, and Camel, were test-marketed. Camel was the clear-cut winner, but the animal on the pack bore about as much resemblance to a real camel as did Buck Duke to Reynolds' best friend. In September, Barnum and Bailey's circus arrived in town and Reynolds saw his chance. The dromedary, Old Joe, was his choice, but wouldn't stand still for the photographer. His trainer gave him a belt across the nose, producing this odd eyes shut, tail up pose, which was immortalized on the pack that would become the best selling cigarette in the world. A lot of Americans who grew up in the first two-thirds of the twentieth century still believe that a camel has only one hump.

Courtesy of the Frank Jones Collection

Progress was the byword in the city's early days, and continued into the twentieth century. As soon as the equipment was available, Winston's businessmen took advantage of improvements. Here, one of C. M. Thomas' new chain-drive trucks hauls a load of Dixie Gem Coal.

Courtesy of the Frank Jones Collection

By 1904, Winston's second water works was ready to go into operation, with modern pumps and a new steel reservoir. But the old brick reservoir, built in the form of a truncated pyramid by the Winston Water Company in 1881, was still being used. Early on the morning of November 2, a Wednesday, the north wall of the pyramid suddenly collapsed, and tons of water poured down the Trade Street hill toward the railroad tracks. It was all over in a few moments time. Nine people were dead and a like number hurt, some seriously. Crowds of citizens gathered at the site to examine the rubble of the reservoir and the splintered remains of houses and sheds. It became known as Winston's worst catastrophe. The city rebuilt most of the houses and paid the costs of medical care and burials. But those who survived would never forget the night the reservoir burst.

Courtesy of the Frank Jones Collection

In October 1904, Winston's Second Water Works, located near the intersection of Oak and Eleventh Streets, began operation. The clear-water basin and pumping house are shown here.

Courtesy of Historic Winston

Winston's first post office stood for only eight years. In 1914, this massive building, a product of the so-called "Federal" style in government buildings, opened on the site of the first one, on Fifth Street between Liberty and Trade. The building is little changed today, except that a later addition put the steps seen on Liberty Street indoors.

Courtesy of the Frank Jones Collection

For the first half-century, Winston's post office moved around quite a bit. In the 1880s, it was located for a time in the courthouse, and in 1891 it was on the east side of Liberty Street just above Fourth. By the turn of the century it had moved to the Lemly building on Main Street, at the southeast corner of Third. But in 1899, the separate post offices of Winston and Salem were consolidated, leaving Salem a branch station, and it was time for a permanent home. In 1906 the new Federal Building, housing the United States Attorney, Commissioner, Deputy Marshall and Internal Revenue Service as well as the Post Office, opened its doors at the corner of Liberty and Fifth. Going north on Liberty past the post office, the next building housed T. A. Brown's bowling alley on the first floor and above, the Jones Building, realty and law offices. Next was the Hippodrome, a vaudeville house. The first church steeple was that of the Centenary Methodist Episcopal Church, the second, the Methodist Protestant Church, on the corner of Seventh. The building in the distance, where Liberty turns to the northeast, was occupied by the A. G. Logan and Company furniture company. Winston-Salem's first post office was an excellent example of incompetent planning and wasteful destruction that infects local planners to this day. In 1914, after only eight years of use, the building was destroyed to make room for a bigger Federal Building.

Courtesy of Bill East

On February 14, 1906, the Carnegie Public Library opened at the corner of Cherry and Third Streets, its shelves stocked with books from the West End School. W. A. Whitaker checked out the first book. The building was erected with a twenty-five thousand dollar grant from Andrew Carnegie, secured by the diligence of J. C. Buxton and others. It was replaced in the 1950s by a spacious, modern building on West Fifth Street, and the old building was acquired by a Catholic Church. The new library was able to provide services made impossible by the cramped quarters of the old one, but that very coziness, enhanced by the twisting maze of book-laden shelves, provides moments of nostalgia for those who were lucky enough to patronize Winston's first library.

Courtesy of Bill East

Following a fund-raising drive in 1906 headed by Robert C. Norfleet, the Y.M.C.A. constructed, in 1907-08, the building on the right at the corner of Fourth and Cherry Streets. The building cost about fifty-thousand dollars and served until it was torn down in 1926 to make way for the Nissen Building. In 1909, the town of Winston got its first separate high school facility, at the left, on Cherry Street. After the school building burned in 1923, the property was acquired by the First Presbyterian Church.

Courtesy of Bill East

When the towns joined together, so did the two police forces. Winston-Salem's first combined department poses for this 1913 photograph. Left to right, front row: Luther W. Kimball, formerly chief of the Salem force, chief James A. Thomas, and A. Columbus Wall. Second row: E. Frank Apple, who operated a meat market on the side with his partner G. W. Hester, Robert W. Bryant, and Robert Young. Third row: Robert L. Blackburn and John T. Thompson, a veteran of more than twenty years. Back row: Norman B. Williams and sanitary inspector Charles A. Pratt. In the 1918 race riot, patrolman Young was killed while trying to help repel the lynch mob in front of the municipal building.

Courtesy of Winston-Salem Police Department

When a fire is discovered, someone calls the fire department and then everyone stands around, listening as the sound of distant sirens grows. On January 30, 1908, the fire was nearer the fire station than it was to the call box at Liberty and Fourth. Even though the firemen had only to cross the street, they were too late. From the old Wachovia Bank building, now the Government Center, we can watch with the usual crowd as Brown, Rogers and Company and F. C. Brown and Sons go up in flames. The firefighters were successful in protecting the City Hall and other nearby buildings from destruction, but a business of thirty years was gone. Within the year, a new building was up for business as usual.

Courtesy of Bill East

The spring of 1912 brought torrential rains to the Atlantic coast of the United States. From New England to Georgia creeks and rivers rose to record heights. On the Southern Railroad operations came to a standstill. Salem Creek, above, backing up from the swollen Yadkin River, spilled over its banks on March 15 and formed a seven hundred foot wide pond at the foot of the Main Street hill. The streetcars were unable to cross to Waughtown, stranding many Southside residents in Salem. Among the businesses pictured, C. E. Krouse and Company, Salem Supply Company, and Meyers Grocery Company suffered the worst damage. Many bridges across the county were washed away, and most of the factories in Winston shut down to conserve water, the water works of both towns having been damaged. The flood got second billing in the newspaper, however, because on that same day the famous Allen clan stormed into the courthouse at nearby Hillsville, Virginia, and killed the judge, the solicitor, and the sheriff, while wounding nine others. They made for the hills, there to be hunted by the largest posse ever assembled along the North Carolina-Virginia border. The story was front page news for nearly a month as one by one members of the family gave themselves up until only the patriarch, Sidna Allen, and a young nephew were left.

Courtesy of Bill East

In 1909, the Methodist Church purchased the old Davis Military Academy site on Sugar Hill. They renovated the remaining buildings and began operation of the Children's Home for orphans and other children in need of decent housing and care. The children contributed a great deal to their own upkeep by operating an ever-expanding farm, one of the largest in the area. The above photo, taken shortly after the opening, shows one of the streets with its row of dormitories.

Courtesy of Bill East

The City Memorial Hospital replaced, in 1914, the old Twin-City Hospital. In 1922 the north wing, at left, was built to accommodate black patients. Two years later, the south wing was completed, both wings being named for R. J. Reynolds, whose estate furnished the funds for their construction. The hospital was one of the city's early fire-proof buildings. The multitude of later additions have left this view unrecognizable today.

Courtesy of the Frank Jones Collection

Dr. William O. Spencer began his practice on Third Street near the Presbyterian Church. Just before the First World War he opened this private sanitarium at the corner of Liberty and Second Streets. The area occupied by the Sheriff's department in the new Hall of Justice corresponds with the first floor of the sanitarium.

Courtesy of the Frank Jones Collection

Given the right circumstances, small towns grow up. Part of the process is the addition of cultural organizations and activities. Before World War I, Winston-Salem was well on its way in that category. One cultural organization was the Monday Afternoon Book Club, pictured above on the steps of Dr. H. Stokes Lott's home at 130 North Cherry. Seated from left to right are Mrs. Alice Maslin (William H.), Mrs. Emma C. Bahnson (Dr. Henry T.), Mrs. Sue Jones (Judge Erastus Beverly), Mrs. Dorcas A. Lott (Dr. H. Stokes), Mrs. Neal Henderson, and president, Mrs. Nettie McIver (Henry E.). Standing: Mrs. Julia Smoak (William W.), Miss Delphine Carter, Mrs. Anna deSchweinitz Fries (Francis H.), Mrs. Robert W. Gorrell, Miss Louise Barber, Mrs. Bess Gray Plumly (Charles), Mrs. Kate Bitting Reynolds (William Neal), Mrs. Abegail Roan (Henry), and Mrs. Lucy B. Patterson (Lindsay). The Monday Afternoon Book Club always met on Tuesday.

Courtesy of the Frank Jones Collection

Nine years after the City Memorial Hospital opened its doors, the city got a fine private hospital, an institution that would assure the best in medical care for local citizens in the years to come. On a tree-washed knoll on Hawthorne Road, the North Carolina Baptist Hospital began operations in 1923 in this five and one-half story brick building. By the 1970s, with its attached Bowman Gray School of Medicine, the hospital would have devoured several entire blocks of residential lots, creating traffic and parking problems that aroused the ire of its neighbors. Understandable as that might be, the reassurance of complete medical assistance in time of crisis weighed heavily on the hospital's side.

Courtesy of the Frank Jones Collection

Dr. Simon Green Atkins, a graduate of St. Augustine Normal and Collegiate Institute, was the founder of the education movement in Winston's black community. In 1891, he established the Columbia Heights neighborhood, with the express purpose of beginning an educational center for blacks. In 1892, the Slater Industrial Academy opened there, with Dr. Atkins as principal. Three years later, the school received official state recognition, and in 1897 the name was changed to the Slater Industrial and State Normal School. In 1905, Slater began offering teaching certificates, and twenty years later, its name changed to Winston-Salem Teacher's College, was authorized to grant the baccalaureate.

Professor Atkins and his wife pose with the 1915 Slater student body. First row, left to right: fourth, Breen Reynolds (Williams); fifth, Irma Neal (Henry); sixth, Nellie Hairston (Bausman). Melvin Dancer and Clyde McKnight are seated at right. Second row: second, Ethel Mebane; sixth, Marjorie Hobson. Third row: first, Marshall Sheppard. Fourth row: first, Leroy Hall; third, Ralph Lanier; fourth, Robert Brown.

Dr. Atkins taught at Livingstone before coming to Winston and was Secretary of Education for the American Methodist Episcopal Zion Church. He took an interest in all areas affecting the welfare of the black community. Around the turn of the century, inspired by a visit to Winston by Booker T. Washington, and in conjunction with Drs. Hall, Jones, and Hargrave, and R. J. Reynolds, he helped to open the Slater Hospital, the first such establishment for blacks in the city, on the Academy grounds. When the first modern high school for blacks opened in Winston-Salem in 1931, it was named the Simon G. Atkins High School, honoring a man dedicated to the education and advancement of his race. Dr. Atkins' sons have continued that tradition in service to Winston-Salem State University, the bloom that sprang from their father's seed.

Courtesy of Mrs. Myrtle Hairston Stepp

In the second decade of the twentieth century, the Twin City's rapid advance in population and increasing demands for education from the black community conspired to create a building boom in the school system. A third factor, consolidation of the two cities, brought about the opening of three schools in 1913 alone.

The first Woodland Avenue Colored Grade School opened in 1910 near the corner of Eleventh. S. A. Smith was the principal.

Courtesy of Historic Winston

In 1911, the North Grade School, T. H. Cash, principal, opened at 906 Patterson Avenue.

Courtesy of Historic Winston

The East Grade School, on Highland at Seventh Street, was completed in 1912. Miss Ada Roan was principal.

Courtesy of Historic Winston

1913 saw three new public schools begin operations. The Oak Street Colored School, J. W. Paisley, principal, stood at 1042 Oak.

Courtesy of Historic Winston

The Central Grade School, formerly the second Salem Boy's School, opened in 1913 on Church at the corner of Bank Street. Miss Annie Wiley was principal. Today the building houses offices of the Moravian Church and the Moravian Book Store.

Courtesy of Historic Winston

Dr. S. G. Atkins, principal of the Slater Academy and State Normal School, took on additional duties as principal of Columbia Heights Colored Grade School at its opening in 1913. His burden was eased somewhat by his assistant principal, Mrs. Lillie Mebane. The building was located on Wallace Street at the corner of Bruce.

Courtesy of Historic Winston

Finally, in 1914, the inadequate frame structure at the corner of Eleventh Street was replaced by the new two-story brick Woodland Avenue Colored Grade School near the corner of Twelfth. R. W. Brown, the principal, found himself teaching in one of the most modern facilities for blacks in the South.

Courtesy of Historic Winston

In 1905 R. J. Reynolds married his cousin,
Mary Catherine Smith of Mt. Airy. She was a woman
of fine intelligence, and would later become one of
Winston-Salem's greatest benefactors. It was her love
of country living that prompted R. J. R. to build the
Reynolda farm. She oversaw the farm and gardens
and took an interest in the welfare of the entire area.
She paid for most of the paving of Reynolda Road
from Stratford to her home and was instrumental in
the development of both the city and county schools.
After Reynolds' death, she married John Edward
Johnston of Philadelphia.

Courtesy of Reynolda House

Posing on the Massachusetts Highway in 1907 with
their chauffeur and nurse are R. J. Reynolds, his wife
Catherine Smith, and their first child, Dick.

Courtesy of Reynolda House

142

The Twin-City Concert Band poses on the steps on the west side of Forsyth County's second courthouse in 1900. By number they are: (1.) Ralph Siewers, Jr. (2.) Fred Fogle, (3.) Charles Woollen, director, (4.) Zack Burton, (5.) Sam Pfohl, (6.) Ed Mickey, (7.) Sam Peterson, (8.) Glenn Woollen, (9.) Harry Mickey, (10.) Robert Walker, (11.) Ed Butner, (12.) Unidentified, (13.) Hal Hayes, (14.) Luther Walker, (15.) Henry Foy, (16.) Walter Crouse, (17.) Jim Peterson. (18.) Samuel T. Mickey, of Civil War fame, (19.) Paul Fogle, (20.) Robert Mickey, (21.) June B. Goslen.

Courtesy of the Frank Jones Collection

The Salem Easter Band on the steps of Salem College's Main Hall in 1903. First row: Bernie Pfohl, Ralph Siewers, Franz Lawson, Agnew Bahnson, Harry Mickey, Fred Fogle, Rufus Schultz. Second row: Hope Holland, Henry Foy, Charles Johnson, Samuel T. Mickey, James Kapp, Ed Mickey, Sam Pfohl, Bernie Wurreschke. Third row: Walter Hege, Charles Woollen, William Peterson, Ernest Stockton, Clyde Rights, Junias Goslen, Paul Fogle, James Peterson. The torch bearers are Horace Vance, Sam Welfare, Charles Vogler, Shirley Rogers, Clarence Leinbach.

Courtesy of the Frank Jones Collection

1905 was a big year for public celebration in the Twin City. Here the Salem bandwagon, driven by Oscar Fisher, prepares to lead the parade of the State Firemen's Convention. The museum of the Wachovia Historical Society, formerly the Boys' School (1794) is in the background. Note the grass growing up between the paving stones on Main Street.

Courtesy of the Frank Jones Collection

Holidays meant parades, and in the old days everyone got into the act. Around 1910, Civil War veterans, above, march down Liberty from Fourth, while below, the school children parade on Third, the girls decked out in summer white and the boys in knickers and cloth caps. The ladies and gentlemen of the town turned out in their buggies and carriages. Note especially the liveried, top-hatted drivers. Music was supplied by the Twin-City concert band and the Gold Leaf Cornet Band, made up of citizens of the black community.

Courtesy of the Frank Jones Collection

After the Mexican War, Anna Morrison attended Salem Female Academy. Later she would marry the astonishing Thomas J. "Stonewall" Jackson, a man of whom General Lee, after Chancellorsville, would say, "I have lost my right arm." In 1914, Anna Morrison Jackson, a widow for fifty years, returned to Salem to receive an honorary degree. Mrs. Jackson is seen here, center, on the arm of Dr. Henry T. Bahnson, himself a Civil War veteran. At left is Bishop Edward Rondthaler, and in the right foreground is the commencement speaker from New York. Behind him is industrialist Henry W. Fries.

Courtesy of Bill East

The Salem band poses on the campus of Salem College in 1912. They are, from left to right, first row: Robert Ormsby, William Ellis, Ralph Pfaff, Henry Hanes, Raiford Porter, Raymond Miller. Second row: Douglas Rights, Clarence Leinbach, John D. Stockton, Clyde Rights, Charlie Vance, Fred Meinung, Francis Grunert. Third row: Sam Brewer, Ollie Peddycord, Harry Mickey, Sidney Brietz, Jim Peterson, Bill Vogler, Clarence Ledford, Walter L. Kern, William Miller, Bernard J. Pfohl, Bill Dugan, Ervin Porter.

Courtesy of the Frank Jones Collection

146

Ernie Shore served thirty-four years as sheriff of Forsyth County. In 1913 he and Babe Ruth, also a pitcher at that time, joined the Boston Red Sox as rookies. Each was given a trial start, and Shore, having shown more stuff, made the starting rotation, becoming the only big league player ever to beat Babe Ruth out of a job. Ruth and Shore roomed together for some time, and it was said that Ernie was the only one who could handle the Babe when he lost his temper. Shore had several fine seasons with the Red Sox before a sore arm and World War I combined to end his career. Here Shore, third from the left, and his Red Sox teammates watch the birdie for the Babe, right, at Boston's Fenway Park.

Courtesy of Ernie G. Shore

In 1914, E. W. O'Hanlon began construction of Winston-Salem's second "skyscraper." Completed in 1915 on the corner of Fourth and Liberty that had come to bear the O'Hanlon name, the building stretched to eight stories with a mezzanine on the ground floor. For two years it would reign as the city's tallest structure. A short time after its completion, the "Human Fly" visited the city and dazzled a large crowd by scaling Winston-Salem's third steel frame building.

Courtesy of the Frank Jones Collection

World War
and the Great Depression 1914-1941

When the United States finally entered the First World War in the Spring of 1917, doughboys embarking for European ports carried with them R. J. Reynolds' new Camel cigarettes. In Winston-Salem, Captain J. G. Wooten's Forsyth Riflemen were just becoming comfortable as civilians after seven months of phantom duels with Pancho Villa on the Mexican border when the order for mobilization came. They put on their uniforms and began recruiting. But they were still en route to the front when eighteen-year-old Private Clyde Bolling, the first local boy to die in the war, fell near Cantigny in the spring of 1918. The Riflemen, along with other Twin Citians, served in the Thirtieth Division, seeing action in the grim stalemate near Ypres and participating in the victorious Meuse-Argonne offensive. Other contingents from Winston-Salem saw action with the Second at Soissons and the Eighty-First at Verdun.

On the home front, the rationing was not severe and Liberty Bond drives were popular and successful. The Board of Aldermen voted funds for six city parks, with Hanes Park becoming the flagship of the system. A year earlier the city had hired a probation officer to deal with juvenile delinquents, and the first county-operated tuberculosis sanitorium in North Carolina had opened outside the city limits. But things were not as good as they seemed to be.

In 1917, for the first time, blacks had been accepted in considerable numbers into regular fighting units, giving many of them a better sense of self-worthiness. And at home, most of the jobs left vacant by young white recruits were filled by blacks, precipitating a mass migration of blacks into the towns and cities. With many of the best young men of both races away in Europe, tensions became severe in the affected urban areas. The end of the war would see race riots sweep a number of American cities. The worst occurred in the north, with Chicago and Cleveland having some of the severest trouble, but Winston-Salem was not to be spared.

On a Sunday afternoon in November 1918, in the midst of a disastrous flu epidemic, a crowd of angry whites began gathering around the City Hall at Main and Fourth Streets. The gathering soon became a lynch mob numbering nearly two thousand. The target was a black man held in the city jail, charged with raping a white woman. White civic leaders urged the mob to disperse. P. H. Hanes had his face bloodied by a thrown piece of coal for his trouble. The mob stormed the jail and was repelled by the Home Guard, which then turned fire hoses on the gathering.

Shooting broke out, and the corner of Fourth and Main quickly became littered with the bodies of the killed and wounded. A fireman, a Home Guardsman, and a thirteen-year-old girl were dead and more than twenty wounded.

The mob then surged into the black sections of town, where the sputter of gun fire could be heard through the night until troops summoned by Mayor Gorrell arrived and parked their tank on the courthouse square. The number of casualties will never be known. Death certificates were filed for five white men and one black, George Johnson, a twenty-two year old machinery hand at R. J. Reynolds Tobacco Company. Eyewitnesses, including one man on duty at the jail that night, state that bodies of a number of blacks were stuffed into railroad culverts or thrown into Belo's Pond. Estimates of the number of blacks killed range as high as fifty, although a somewhat lower number is more likely.

Fifteen white men received sentences of from fourteen months to six years on the county roads. One black man, Will Davis, was executed for the murder of a Southern Public Utilities Company worker. The original target of the mob was found not guilty of rape on the testimony of the victim.

By 1915, R. J. Reynolds had enlarged their oldest factory, number 256, and constructed another, number eight. In that year, with sales of the new Camel cigarettes beginning to boom, they built their third and largest factory, number twelve, on Chestnut Street. The building at the right in this 1916 photograph housed the Reynolds Inn, built to provide decent accommodations for single girls working in the plants. Reynolds is still using all three of its oldest plants.

Courtesy of Bill East

Sometime before four a.m. on the morning of April 27, 1916, fire broke out in the kitchen of the Neil Hotel on Liberty Street. It quickly spread to the Elk's Auditorium next door, at the corner of Fifth. All fire companies in Winston-Salem, including the R. J. Reynolds Tobacco Company's private unit, responded to the alarms. By five a.m. the boarding house behind the auditorium, operated by Reynolds for its employees, had also caught. By the time it was all over, the hotel and auditorium were smoking ruins and the Cash Barber Shop, Hutchins' Drug Store, and Liberty Billiard Parlor were so badly damaged that they had to be torn down. Damage was estimated at ninety thousand dollars. The auditorium was rebuilt on the spot, later becoming the State Theatre, where generations of children would thrill to Saturday morning shoot 'em-ups and cliff-hanging serials. Still later the building was used as a furniture store until it was torn down in 1973 to make way for a parking deck.

Courtesy of Bill East

In 1919 other troubles plagued the Twin City. Harking back to the Single Brothers' rebellion in 1778, local workers began to unionize. Strikes or threats of strikes menaced virtually every manufacturing concern in town. Some few succeeded, but like the Single Brothers, R. J. Reynolds' workers were steamrolled into submission. And the city fathers went on another building binge. By 1929 Winston-Salem had seven skyscrapers, creating a skyline that would remain unchanged until the middle of the century.

The suburbs began to sprout. The first influx into Ardmore had started before the war. Before the depression put a stop to new building, more than a thousand homes would be built there. Reynolda was a thriving village with its own separate post office and black community, called Five Row. As Ardmore continued to expand other suburbs grew up around it and development was begun in Buena Vista. By the time of the Wall Street fiasco in 1929, the growing prosperity of the black lawyers, doctors, churchmen, and educators created a demand for middle-class housing. They built Alta Vista along West Twenty-Fifth Street, the first black restricted neighborhood in the south.

Prosperity was the hallmark of the times. National prohibition had come in 1919, but North Carolina had been legally dry for a decade, and those who wanted a drink knew how to find it. Henry Ford put the price of his automobiles within the reach of most, but the streets of Winston-Salem served more than their share of the higher priced cars from Cadillac, Stutz, and Pierce. A transportation revolution was underway. Experience gained in the recently completed war made commercial aviation a viable commodity. The first airplane to arrive in Winston-Salem had landed in a pasture on the Hanes Farm, near where the roads to Clemmons and Lewisville branched. Shortly thereafter, Twin Citians erected Maynard Field, one of the first municipal airports in the South.

Such progressive thinking attracted new business enterprises. In 1923, Security Life and Trust Company moved its offices from Greensboro to Winston-Salem, and the North Carolina Baptist Hospital opened on Hawthorne Road. The following year Ralph P. Hanes, a pretty good polo player, opened Hanes Dye and Finishing Company, destined to become the largest firm of its type in the world.

Baseball was the American game and aviation was the American enterprise. In 1927, Lucky Lindy flew the Atlantic and Babe Ruth hit sixty home runs. Winston-Salem was not to be outdone. Young Dick Reynolds and his baby brother, Zachary Smith, were already beginning to make names for themselves at the controls of those popular flying machines. Hometown boy Alvin Floyd Crowder was still learning the big league hitters that year, but in 1928 he led the St. Louis Browns into third place with a brilliant twenty-one and five record. He would go on to post 167 major league wins with the Browns, the Washington Nationals, and the Detroit Tigers, pitching in three World Series along the way. He was called "The General," and in his best year he won twenty-six games for the 1932 Nationals.

On the local scene in 1927 the Salem Steel Company opened and the tallest building in North Carolina, the Nissen Building, was completed. Also that year an act of the General Assembly transferred the West Bend-Panther Creek area from Yadkin to Forsyth County, ending a years long struggle to make the Yadkin River Forsyth's western boundary.

When the stock market came apart in 1929, the building boom began to fade. At the low point of the Great Depression nearly ten thousand Twin Citians were existing entirely on public relief funds. Some who had flocked to the city during the industrial expansion went back to the farm. But Winston-Salem was luckier than many cities and towns. The industrial concerns cut back their production, but none of the major ones closed altogether, except the Chatham Manufacturing Company, which decided to consolidate its operations in Elkin. It was a grim time, but the citizens of the town pushed on.

In 1930 Winston-Salem got its first radio station and the majestic Moravian Easter Sunrise Service was carried live on the air for the first time. The Civic Music Association and a Public Recreation Commission were formed, and Summit School, lured by Reynolds money, moved from its old home in the West End to a lush woodland setting at Reynolda.

As the depression began to ease, the people of Winston-Salem could again look forward to what they hoped would be years of peace and prosperity. They would get the prosperity but it would be bought at dear price. As W. P. A. funds were put to use in building a new stadium and paving and extending city

streets, Adolph Hitler's legions were girding themselves for a strike into the heart of Europe. And while planning went ahead for the establishment of the Bowman Gray School of Medicine in 1941, the Japanese admiralty was doing some planning of its own, of a quite different sort. But the people of the Twin Cities had been through too much and wanted no part of the coming war. While Hitler was running amuck in Poland and Hungary, local leaders were studying the blueprints for the magnificent new Reynolds Park which would open in 1940.

Grover C. Jarvis was one of Winston-Salem's early automotive wizards. Here he poses, right, with the electric car he created in 1916. The drive mechanism was powered by storage batteries installed in an existing chassis. Around 1917, Mr. Jarvis opened the Jarvis Battery Company at 803 Trade Street, employing Leonard J. Johnson, left, as his first electrician. The company is still in business today, operated by Mr. Jarvis' sons, and in a display case in their offices is a steam engine hand-crafted by Grover Jarvis in his youth.

Courtesy of the Frank Jones Collection

Looking north along Liberty at the intersection with Fourth in the fall of 1918, we find the Marine Corps recruiting tent on the courthouse lawn, seeking enlistees for the war in Europe. But the real interest in town is indicated by the signs proclaiming a "Great October Harvest Sale" at Belk-Stevens Company and "World Series Upstairs." Upstairs at the People's National Bank, in addition to the results of the Boston Red Sox versus Chicago Cubs series, could be found the offices of W. A. and D. H. Blair, attorneys, and Hinshaw & Ziglar, civil engineers, along with the

Moose Home and Woodmen of the World. Beyond Belk-Stevens were The Vogue, men's furnishings, the Phoenix Cafe, and W. T. Vogler and Sons, jewelers. The new O'Hanlon Building (1915) housed, on its ground floor, O'Hanlon's Drug Store, with Hutchins' Drug Store next door. Across Liberty, V. O. Thompson's Drug Store rounded out the pharmaceutical trade. Next to it stood the first store of Frank A. Stith, followed by Smith and Spry, barbers, and the Athens Cafe.

Courtesy of the Frank Jones Collection

R. J. Reynolds, Winston-Salem's greatest industrialist, lived, for his first twenty years in the town, either in his factory or in various hotels and boarding houses. When he married his cousin Catherine Smith in 1905, he had been, for some ten years, sharing a dwelling with his brother and sister-in-law, William Neal and Kate Bitting Reynolds, at 666 West Fifth Street. Catherine was not happy with city life, so around 1918 the couple moved into their new sixty room "Bungalow," right center, designed by Charles Barton Keen of Philadelphia. It was a self-contained village, with its own church, school, and post office, known as Reynolda, North Carolina. The most imposing structure, other than the house itself, was the barn, at left center, although the formal gardens, lower center, landscaped by Thomas Sears of Philadelphia, have endured as the most important aspect of the estate. Wake Forest University now occupies the area above Lake Catherine, while the house, now known as Reynolda House, is a museum. The barn houses shops and the Museum of Man, while the gardens are maintained as one of the city's showplaces.

Courtesy of the Frank Jones Collection

Looking south on Liberty from Third around 1920, the Sentinel Printing and Publishing Company building is visible at the left. Along with job printing, the company produced the *Twin-City Sentinel* and the semi-weekly *Western Sentinel*. Below the *Sentinel* were, in order, the wholesale dry goods concern of Fletcher Brothers Company, the Twin City Motor Company, Barber Printing Company, the offices of Southern Bell Telephone and Telegraph Company, and J. W. B. Comer's confectionery shop. At the right is the Starbuck Building, housing, among others, architects Northup and O'Brien, the Carolina Olds Company, and the Winston Printing Company. The next building below was Powell Gilmer's Salem Motors. The east side of the street is now the site of the Hall of Justice, while the west side accommodates the North Carolina National Bank Plaza.

Courtesy of the Frank Jones Collection

Black businessmen joined in the post-war economic
boom. In April 1918 the owners and employees of the
Morgan and Scales Garage posed in their
establishment at 502 East Fourth Street.

Courtesy of Blanche Morgan Hobson

William Neal Reynolds, brother of R. J., bought a huge parcel of land on the banks of the Yadkin River in 1921. The area had been the site of Fort Johnson during the French and Indian War, and came with an 1859 house and the Mt. Pleasant Methodist Church (1809). Mr. Will built wings onto the old house, installed stables, gardens, and a racetrack where he oversaw the workouts of his horses, two of which won major races. Under terms of his will, "Tanglewood" became a public park, with a swimming pool, boat lake, golf course, and a "barn" theatre. The park was purchased by Forsyth County in early 1977.

Courtesy of the Frank Jones Collection

The First National Bank Building was built in 1919 at the corner of Liberty and Third Streets. Six stories with a basement, and of fire-proof construction, it provided office space on floors one through four, the fifth and sixth floors and basement being used for automobile storage. A later attempt to operate it as a parking deck was foiled by the cumbersome necessity of loading cars into an elevator. The site is now occupied by the North Carolina National Bank Plaza.

Photo by Frank Jones

William Patrick Hairston was born in Virginia in
1876. Around the turn of the century he came to
Winston and began a career in business and civic
affairs, which found him, by 1930, established as
General Agent for Winston Mutual and Secretary of
Fraternal Funeral Directors, Inc. Here he is seen in his
office in the Winston Mutual Building in 1922 with his
fifteen year old son, William H. Hairston.

Courtesy of Myrtle Hairston Stepp

When the first Winston-Salem High School burned in 1923, a new structure was quickly put up on Silver Hill, overlooking Hanes Park and the West End. Catherine Smith Reynolds, widow of R. J. R., put up the money for a magnificent companion auditorium. It was the finest high school plant in the state, with a gilt-edged faculty to match, among them such mainstays in local education as Mary Wiley, Claude R. Joyner, John Watson Moore, and R. S. Haltiwanger. Seeds sown by Calvin Wiley in the nineteenth century would come to fruition with erection of the James A. Gray (1930), John W. Hanes (1930), and Simon A. Atkins (1931) High Schools, giving Winston-Salem the best secondary education system in the South.

Courtesy of the Frank Jones Collection

The Robert E. Lee Hotel operated the Robert E. Lee Taxi and Baggage Transfer Company in the 1920s and 1930s. The hacks would meet all passenger trains at the old depot on Third Street, and later at the new Union Station. In the second car from the right is driver John Adams.

Courtesy of Historic Winston

Robert Gray, Harman Miller, and Francis Fries wouldn't have recognized their town in 1925. Looking north on Liberty from Fourth the only familiar sight would have been the steeple of Centenary Methodist Epispocal Church. Next to E. W. O'Hanlon's drugstore and office building at left, the Woolworth Building, housing on its first floor G. R. Kenney's shoe store and the Woolworth "five and dime," had replaced D. D. Schouler's "Racket Store." Upstairs, young Archie Elledge had his law office. Next came Watkins' Book Store and Sosnik and Sosnik, ladies' clothing. The Farmer's Warehouse had been replaced by the Merchant's Bank and Trust Building, adorned with a poster heralding the coming of John Robinson's Circus.

On the right, next to where Mr. Miller had put up the first store in Winston, stood the United Retail Drug Company and the United Cigar Store building, with Spry's Barber Shop as a tenant. Farther down the block the Rominger Furniture Company was flanked by the Ideal and Colonial Theatres, where a parking deck now stands.

Courtesy of the Frank Jones Collection

That a demand for wagons existed into the late twenties is evidenced by this aerial view of the G. E. Nissen Wagon Works on Waughtown Street between Tryon and Marble Streets. Across the street is the Waughtown Baptist Church. In less than a decade motor transport would have made the streetcar tracks on Waughtown obsolete, and the wagon works, having barely observed its centennial, would be a thing of the past.

Courtesy of the Frank Jones Collection

With plans underway to sell the old municipal building property, the need arose for a new city market. Temporary quarters were found in a former R. J. Reynolds Tobacco Company building on Cherry Street, while construction was begun on the new market in 1924. Completed in 1925 at the corner of Cherry and Sixth, the Market was less specialized than the old one, offering fresh country butter and sausage, cut flowers, cured hams, and a wide variety of vegetables in season. The delicious range of smells is one of the earliest childhood memories of many a Twin Citian.

Courtesy of the Frank Jones Collection

In the 1920s, Winston-Salem provided a market sufficient to attract regional and national chain stores. The year 1925 saw a Woolworth store already in operation, and on Fourth Street, opposite the courthouse, sidewalk superintendents turned out to oversee the construction of the new home of Raylass Chain Stores, "1¢ to $1.00." It would be flanked by, at left, the Henry Clay Shoe Store and the United Retail Drug Company and United Cigar Store Company. On the right the Winston Clothing Company held the ground floor, while above were the offices of a lawyer, tailor, Justice of the Peace, the Brotherhood of Railroad Trainmen number 433, and the Knights of Pythias Damon Lodge number 41. Already, no one could remember who had operated the "Parisian Dressmaking" establishment recalled by the out-of-date sign.

Courtesy of the Frank Jones Collection

Fourth Street runs diagonally from left to right across
the center of this aerial view, taken from the southwest
just before the transformation of the downtown area.
Within months, the second county courthouse (1897)
and the old municipal building (1892), on the square
at the upper right center, would be razed to make way
for the new courthouse (1926) and the R. J. Reynolds
Tobacco Company office building (1929). Along
Fourth Street, the Masonic Temple (1906), at the
corner of Trade; the Y.M.C.A. (1908), at the corner of
Cherry; and the houses at the northwest corner of
Fourth and Marshall, built in the 1880s and 1890s,
would all meet the same fate, to be replaced
respectively by Walgreen's Drug Store (1926), the
Nissen Building (1927), and the Carolina Apartments
and Hotel (1928). Already the Wachovia (1911/1918)
and O'Hanlon (1915) buildings on the square had been
dwarfed by the new Robert E. Lee Hotel (1921) at the
upper left. In the foreground, most of the homes of
Winston's first residential area were still standing. The
only building in that area that remains today is J. W.
Hanes' Shamrock Mills, the distinctive saw-tooth roof
of which can be seen at the lower left.

Courtesy of the Frank Jones Collection

West Fourth Street looking east from Cherry. On the north side from the left are Montaldo's, Brotan's Fifth Avenue Shops of New York, ladies' ready-to-wear and millinery, and E. L. Hine's shoe store, above which was Miss A. H. Allen's art studio. On the south side from the right are W. S. Fisher's cleaning and dyeing establishment and Henry Der Yen's Chinese laundry. The building that today houses the Bank of North Carolina was vacant. East of it were D. G. Craven's department store and the Anchor Company.

Courtesy of Historic Winston

West Fourth Street looking west from Liberty. On the left, at the sign of the boot, is E. E. Hailey's Electric Shoe Shop and Shine Parlor. Between there and Patterson's Cut Rate Drugs are the Rialto Cafe and Nichol's Hat Shop. Beyond Patterson's are Gus Polite's Candy Kitchen, the Amuzu Theatre, and the Alpha Cafe. From the right are the Walk-Over Boot Shop, the Pilot Theatre, Efird's Department Store, and, across Trade Street, the Masonic Temple.

Courtesy of Historic Winston

North Liberty looking south from Fifth Street. Behind the wagon at left is Mear's Jewelry Company. Farther down, near Rominger's Furniture Company, are the Broadway Theatre and the Wall-Huske Hardware Company. From the right are the Ideal Photo Company, Martin McNulty's florist shop, the Liberty Street store of the Frank A. Stith Company, Gilmer's Department Store, the Hawkins Company (dry goods), the Arcade Fashion Shop, Cohen's (ladies' clothing), and the Warner Millinery Company. In the distance can be seen the sign of Belk-Stevens' Department Store on the square.

Courtesy of Historic Winston

North Liberty looking north from Fifth Street. From the left are A. Daye's Sweet Shop, the Crews-Newsom Company, the Central Hotel, and E. J. Angelo's grocery. Through the windshield of the second car can be seen the sign of the Piggly Wiggly Carolina Company, grocers. In the distance is the spire of the Centenary Methodist Episcopal Church. Next to Brown-Rogers-Dixon Hardware at the right is the Home Real Estate Loan and Insurance Company of S. L. Ogburn and T. E. Kapp, still in business today at the same location. A business college occupied the second floor. Next came the offices of the Crystal Ice Company, the Great Atlantic and Pacific Tea Company's Liberty Street Store, the H. H. Jones Furniture Company, and the J. C. Penny Store. At the end of the block was the bus line station operated by J. H. Money and C. M. "Pop" Shouse.

Courtesy of Historic Winston

West Fourth Street looking east from near Spruce Street. The men at left sit on the steps leading to the home of the Reverend Samuel W. Hahn, pastor of Augsburg Lutheran Church, which stood across the street. Across Spruce is the number two service station of the Pilot Motor Service. From the right are Smoak's Drug Store and the Cordon Paint Company. The building near the center housed a miscellany of offices, followed by Twin City Dry Cleaning and Hersh and Silverstein, tailors. On the corner, at center, is the Twin City Club. The block between Marshall and Cherry, awaiting construction of the Nissen Building, is empty. In the background, at the corner of Cherry, is the Realty Building, offices.

Courtesy of Historic Winston

West Fifth Street looking west from Liberty Street. From the left are the offices of Money-Hanner Realty and Insurance Company and Newton Brothers, real estate and rentals. The familiar Frank A. Stith Company arrow marks their Fifth Street store. Beyond Stith's is Barber Photo Supply Company, now Lindley Photo. Next is the Gilmer Company's bakery and dairy lunch, followed by the Post Office Lunch at the corner of Trade. The Post Office Building (1914), is at right.

Courtesy of Historic Winston

The majestic and dignified Moravian Easter Sunrise Service has attracted the attention of visitors in Salem since the first one in 1773. The service has been conducted in every year but one since then. Here, in 1925, the throngs choke Cemetery Street next to God's Acre in anticipation of the festivities comemmorating the moment in which "Christ our Lord is risen today." The music of the Moravian bands begins to wake the townspeople in the early morning hours and reaches its glorious and touching peak as the sun sends its first gleams darting into the ancient graveyard of the Unitas Fratrum.

Courtesy of the Frank Jones Collection

Before the advent of national radio, the latest information on national events was available only at the local newspaper office. Here a crowd of baseball fans gathers in front of Powell Gilmer's Salem Motor Company, dealers in Maxwell and Chrysler automobiles, on Liberty below Third, to follow the second game of the 1926 World Series between the New York Yankees and the St. Louis Cardinals. The *Sentinel* had an elaborate "Playograph" display that listed the lineups and, by mechanical means, operated by the proudest boy in town, could show the play-by-play progress of the game. In 1926, the mighty Yankees were heavy favorites. Babe Ruth hit three home runs in the Series, but the aging Grover Cleveland Alexander, an alcoholic thought to be washed up, pitched brilliantly, winning two games and coming in to strike out Tony Lazerri with the bases loaded to save the seventh game, and the Series, for the Cardinals. The local system was good for everybody, for in a slack moment an eager young salesman might be able to sell a car.

Courtesy of the Frank Jones Collection

The coming of the horseless carriage brought changes in public transportation. In 1912, O. A. Kirkman began a jitney service to High Point with a steam-drive vehicle. By the mid-twenties, jitnies serving surrounding counties were being operated by Pop Shouse (Yadkin), Tom Caudle (Wilkes), and Ernest P. Walker (Davie). Locally, the black community, left off the streetcar lines, had its own service, supplied by such pioneers as E. A. Davis, G. F. Ragsdale, E. T. Miller, and I. Boyd Holden. In 1926, the black operators combined, forming Safe Bus, Incorporated, for local transport. The first officers were H. F. Morgan, president; J. H. Hairston, vice-president; and C. R. Peebles, secretary. That same year, John L. Gilmer bought up a number of inter-county jitney services and began the Camel City Coach Company, which merged in 1930 with the Blue and Gray Lines of West Virginia to form the Atlantic Greyhound Lines.

Courtesy of Historic Winston

Before Safe Bus acquired adequate space, the buses were parked each night in front of Ralph R. Hairston's home at 1424 Cromartie Street. Beginning with a fleet of thirty-five buses and a city-wide five-cent fare, the undertaking met with immediate success. In 1941 the firm acquired controlling interest in Camel City Cab, Incorporated. By 1947 they were operating 48 buses and 36 taxicabs, and employing 146 persons; the combined payroll exceeded a quarter of a million dollars. At the left is the home of J. F. Dudley, who operated a shoe repair business.

Courtesy of Blanche Morgan Hobson

C. T. WOODLAND
Vice-President

R. R. MORGAN
Vice-President

E. T. MILLER
Secretary

J. H. HAIRSTON
Treasurer

Officers of Safe Bus in 1935 included the above men. President of the company at that time was C. R. Peebles.

Courtesy of Blanche Morgan Hobson

JITNEY LINE

BETWEEN

Columbia Heights and City

H. F. MORGAN (Proprietors
R. R. MORGAN (

MORNING SCHEDULE

Leave Columbian Heights	Leave City
6 30 o'clock	7 00 o'clock
7 10 "	7 30 "
7 30 "	7 40 "
7 40 "	7 55 "
7 55 "	8 10 "
8 10 "	8 25 "
8 25 "	8 40 "
8 40 "	9 15 "
9 05 "	9 45 "
9 35 "	10 20 "
10 00 "	10 50 "
10 40 "	11 30 "
11 20 "	
11 50 "	

One of Safe Bus' predecessors was the well organized Jitney Line of H. F. and R. R. Morgan, both later officers of Safe Bus. Their schedule is reproduced here.

Courtesy of Blanche Morgan Hobson

In 1910 construction was begun on a nine-hole golf course on the Shallowford (Country Club) Road. Within a few years nine more holes were finished, and the Forsyth County Club was a success. In 1929, the suburban golf club was merged with the downtown Twin City Club. Nine years later the Old Town Club began operation on the edge of the Reynolds Estate at the end of Kent Road, and within a few more years, the original suburban club was again independent, its name changed to the Forsyth Country Club. Forsyth's first clubhouse is shown below.

Photo by Frank Jones

Circuses have always been popular attractions, dating back to the days when the now defunct Browntown, near Union Cross, was a center for circus activities. Here a horsedrawn parade makes its way along Twenty-Fifth Street near Liberty in the early part of this century.

Courtesy of the Frank Jones Collection

J. B. McCreary, who, with W. W. Smoak, operated Winston's largest livery business in the early 1900s, was elected high sheriff of Forsyth County in 1922. During his administration, the county got its first motorcycle officers. On the lawn of the new courthouse (1926), they are, from left to right, Ken Pfaff, Mack Spainhour, and A. C. Bovender. The sheriff's department did not get automobiles until the late thirties under Ernie Shore, deputies having to supply their own vehicles until that time.

Courtesy of the Frank Jones Collection

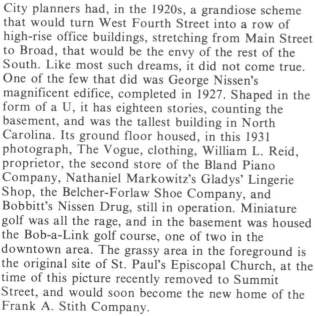

City planners had, in the 1920s, a grandiose scheme that would turn West Fourth Street into a row of high-rise office buildings, stretching from Main Street to Broad, that would be the envy of the rest of the South. Like most such dreams, it did not come true. One of the few that did was George Nissen's magnificent edifice, completed in 1927. Shaped in the form of a U, it has eighteen stories, counting the basement, and was the tallest building in North Carolina. Its ground floor housed, in this 1931 photograph, The Vogue, clothing, William L. Reid, proprietor, the second store of the Bland Piano Company, Nathaniel Markowitz's Gladys' Lingerie Shop, the Belcher-Forlaw Shoe Company, and Bobbitt's Nissen Drug, still in operation. Miniature golf was all the rage, and in the basement was housed the Bob-a-Link golf course, one of two in the downtown area. The grassy area in the foreground is the original site of St. Paul's Episcopal Church, at the time of this picture recently removed to Summit Street, and would soon become the new home of the Frank A. Stith Company.

Courtesy of the Frank Jones Collection

Having survived nearly three-quarters of a century, J. E. Mickey's old coffee pot stood watch over the changes on Main Street in 1927. At left the porch of H. E. Nissen's house is discernable, next to the expanding quarters of Frank Vogler and Son, funeral directors, dating from the same period. The coffee pot was finally moved to make way for Interstate Forty in the 1950s, while Vogler's continues in the same location, having added branches on Reynolda Road and in Clemmons. The houses at right, behind which the new City Hall is seen as a dark bulk, were later torn down for a parking lot.

Courtesy of the Frank Jones Collection

In December 1919, Winston-Salem's first municipal airport, Maynard Field, opened on the old Kernersville Road, near the present Maynard Drive. A few years later, the city combined with Greensboro and High Point to utilize the Tri-City Airport, at Friendship, now the site of the Greensboro-High Point-Winston-Salem Airport. Inspired by Charles Lindbergh and the feats of local fly-boys Dick and Z. Smith Reynolds, Winston-Salem built its own airport in 1927. Clint Miller gave the materials, grading, and his name to Miller Municipal Airport. A later infusion of Reynolds' money would change its name to the Smith Reynolds Airport.

Courtesy of Bill East

Before television and air conditioning combined to make America an indoor society, people knew how to celebrate a holiday. On Memorial Day, 1929, the Twin City welcomed General Summerall, Army Chief of Staff, with a seventeen-gun salute at the Union Station on Claremont Avenue. At ten a.m. the Clyde Bolling Post Band, marching down Fourth Street, led off a gigantic parade that included Spanish-American and Civil War veterans, a tank, the Fort Bragg Post Band, and a cavalry unit, the Black Horse Troop. After speeches at the Auditorium Theatre, a sham battle was commenced on a hill east of Skyland School. Then the Winston-Salem polo team defeated the team from Fort Bragg, eight to four, at Reynolda Field. Dave Drage and Jim Hanes scored three goals each, while Phin Horton had two. The grand finale came that night at Southside Park, with the Twin City's first professional boxing match. Jack Gross, billed in an article by Frank Spencer as a contender for the vacant heavyweight title, scored a technical knockout over Billy Dugan in the third round of a scheduled ten round main event. It was a big day, and July the Fourth was yet to come.

Courtesy of Bill East

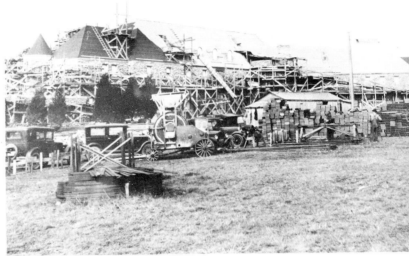

The building boom of the 1920s is graphically illustrated by this 1928 photograph, looking east on Fourth Street from near Poplar. The brand new Nissen Building, at right, oversees the construction of downtown landmarks. At left, the Bocock-Stroud building is nearly ready for occupancy. Across Spruce Street, the F. W. Woolworth building has its framework in place, while farther along, the Carolina Hotel and Apartments rears skyward. In the background the skeleton of the Reynolds Building, which, with the Belo House and the unfortunately destroyed second Forsyth County Court House, make up the three most innovative buildings ever erected in the Twin City, is being filled in. These structures would give Winston-Salem its distinctive skyline, virtually unaltered until the 1960s.

Courtesy of the Frank Jones Collection

Bowman Gray, an early protege of R. J. Reynolds, began construction, in 1928, of a French country mansion on Reynolda Road, across from Reynolds' estate. The firm of Northup and O'Brien called in Luther Lashmit, who was then teaching at Carnegie Tech, to design the wandering sixty-room house. Because of the onset of the depression and death threats directed at the Gray family, construction required nearly four years to complete, but, contrary to persistent local legend, Mr. Gray enjoyed living in his new house from 1932 until his death in 1935.

The controversy centered upon objections to such an arrogant display of wealth while thousands were starving, but the objectors failed to take into account the number of jobs created on the local market by this and other mansion-building projects.

Extensive use was made of reinforced concrete in the walls and floors, and there was an indoor swimming pool adjoining Mr. and Mrs. Gray's private living suites. The buildings and grounds were later given to the Bowman Gray School of Medicine. A portion of the estate now serves as a home for the popular "Music at Sunset" series of outdoor concerts presented by the Winston-Salem Symphony Orchestra.

Courtesy of the Frank Jones Collection

By the time of the Wall Street fiasco, Fourth Street had supplanted Trade, Liberty, and Main as Winston-Salem's center of commercial activity. Looking east in 1938, toward the intersection with Spruce, we find that the depression could not dim the Christmas spirit of the Twin City's "Great White Way." Note the Great Atlantic and Pacific Tea Company's store at left, on the corner of Spruce. The closeup reveals an oasis of entertainment brightly aglow between Spruce and Marshall Streets. After dinner at the Piccadilly, Eddie Cantor strutted his stuff in *Ali Baba Goes to Town* at the Carolina, while the Forsyth countered with the engaging Rosalind Russell. If the *March of Time* and popcorn were not attractive, one might find a leisurely game of eight-ball and a tall, cold one at the General Crowder Billiards.

Photos by Frank Jones

176

The building boom in Ardmore precipitated the need for neighborhood churches. The suburb centered upon a triangle created by its three main thoroughfares, Miller and Academy Streets and Hawthorne Road. Within this triangle, the Ardmore Baptist and Methodist congregations built churches in the 1920s. Then, in 1931, the Moravian congregation erected, at the northeastern apex, the Ardmore Moravian Church, on the corner of Hawthorne and Academy. Academy Street, with the new church near its western terminus and Home Church at the eastern end, provided a comforting symbolic tie to antiquity and tradition for the suburban communicants.

Courtesy of Historic Winston

In April 1935 Winston-Salem's Miller Municipal Airport inaugurated regular air service. The first plane to land, operated by Eastern Air Service, Incorporated, later Eastern Airlines, was this Curtiss Condor, a twin-engined bi-plane designed for passenger and freight service. By the end of the year services were discontinued because of inadequate facilities, and regular air service for the Twin City would not resume until 1941.

Courtesy of Historic Winston

Looking south on Main from near the corner of Sixth we find that there were still trees in the heart of downtown in 1938. The old county jail, somewhat remodeled, was still holding forth near the corner of Fifth, with James L. Matthews as jailor. Next to it stood the City Garage. Among the businesses between the garage and the Reynolds Building were the Gem Billiard Parlor and Herman's Delicatessen. The Brown Derby, a beer hall, stood across the street. The trees are long since gone and there is no parking on Main Street.

Courtesy of the Frank Jones Collection

Before technology brought us the "cherry-picker" and the "snorkel," ingenuity provided the pick-up truck with a bed-mounted scaffold. Here city workmen change burnt-out traffic lights at the corner of Fourth and Marshall in 1938.

Photo by Frank Jones

Despite the slow down in building brought on by the
depression, the Twin-City continued to have a demand
for lumber, as evidenced by this 1938 view of the
Fogle Brothers' lumber yard. Although no longer in
the construction business, the sixty-seven-year-old firm
continued to produce lumber, siding, and molding for
the building trade and is operating today as one of the
city's oldest continuously functioning businesses.

Photo by Frank Jones

The opening of the tobacco sales warehouses, always a festive occasion in the old days, was particularly welcome during the Great Depression. This series of photographs by Frank Jones from the late 1930s depicts the atmosphere of the famous "tobacco break." For many tobacco farmers, the auctions provided the only yearly chance for a visit to town, there to have the sweat and toil of a year's work converted into a little hard cash for the necessities of their families.

Sharp-eyed buyers follow the chant of the auctioneer. His song was so pleasant to the ear that the American Tobacco Company, archenemy of R. J. Reynolds, for years mounted a successful advertising campaign upon it, with the closing line: "Sold to American." A farmer unhappy with the price brought by his leaf might "turn the ticket," thereby refusing the bid, and put his goods up for sale another day. Sometimes a simple matter, like cleaning the hands, would bring on an increase in price.

Three farmers tote, using the approved hand-on-hip method, a cheap and efficient system of motive power.

Hands of tobacco are stacked on circular baskets and
dollied into the warehouse for weighing and grading.
A "hand" consisted of the number of leaves the worker
could hold in one hand while the tier knotted the stem
ends with another leaf.

Inspecting the hands of bright leaf in the warehouse. The sights and sounds and the pungent aroma of cured tobacco are precious memories of childhood for those girls and boys lucky enough to have been there. The coming financial reward for back-breaking hours in the fields was a thing to savor.

The big moment. Farmers enter the "payoff office," a central clearing bureau for Gorrell's, Pepper's, Piedmont, Planter's, George-Davis, and Carolina Central Warehouses.

The influx of tobacco money brought the merchants out on the streets. Here shoes, hats, crisp new overalls, and "Sunday suits" are offered for sale.

Fresh produce is the offering here. "Curb Service" usually meant what it said. Housewives from Ardmore or cooks from Buena Vista might order from their vehicles at curbside, but during the tobacco market, they might not be noticed in the press of bodies on the sidewalk.

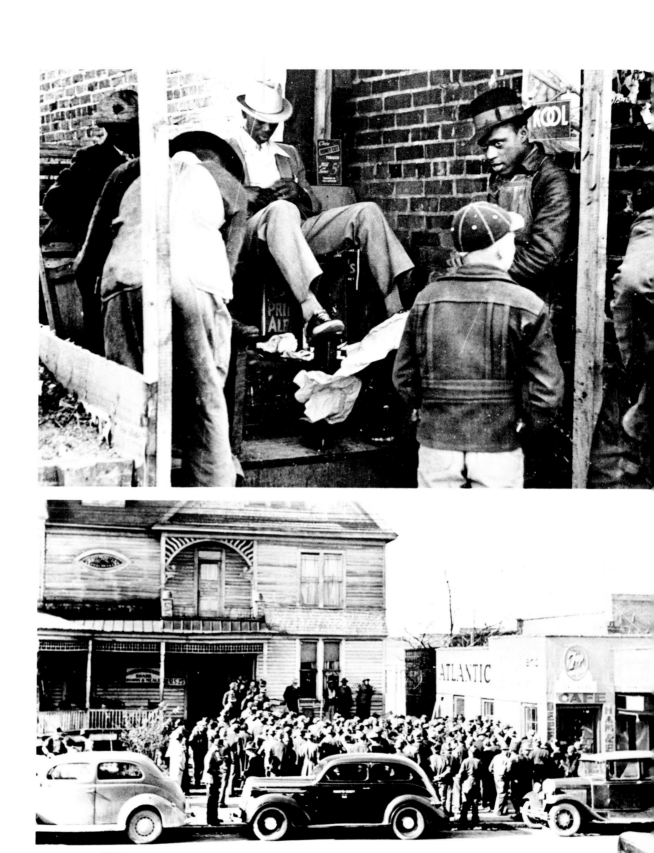

Open air business flourished during the market. The pop of a shoeshine rag, inspiration for "The Chattanooga Shoeshine Boy," could be heard along Trade Street far into the night.

The cash-flow generated by the market attracted the fast-buck artists. Here the barker catches the attention of passing farmers.

An "Indian" wardance to hold the crowd for the pitchman. Down the alley is the product, a patent medicine or...

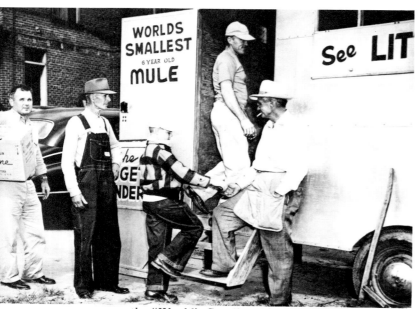

...the "World's Smallest Six-year-old mule," or...

...a portable wax museum, "Great Moments in American History." The sign reflects the times. Along with George Washington are offered the likenesses of Bruno Hauptman, Baby Face Nelson, John Dillinger, "The Girl in Red," Bonnie Parker, and Clyde Barrow. Here our potential customer appears to be skeptical. We can hope he invested any spare cash in I.B.M. or, even better, Disney Productions.

Photos by Frank Jones

Farmers and city-folk alike clog the parking lot of the
City Market in this late-thirties scene. In the
background is the establishment of W. G. White and
Company, noted for their hard candy and country
hams and still in business today as one of the Twin
City's oldest and most respected grocery operations.

Courtesy of the Frank Jones Collection

Reynolds Park, at its opening in 1941, was one of the
finest such municipal facilities in the South. Among its
attractions were a roller rink, a permanent carnival,
and outdoor bowling alleys. Wally G. Dunham was its
first manager.

Courtesy of Historic Winston

The Twin City Comes of Age 1942-Present

The reaction in Winston-Salem on the afternoon of December 7, 1941, was mirrored in every city and town in America. First, shocked disbelief, then anger. Some local men were already in uniform with the various service branches, and in the fall of 1940 the two National Guard companies had been called to active service, but the Japanese attack galvanized the young men of the Twin City into action. Half-deserted recruiting offices found themselves suddenly inundated. Like the doughboys of World War I, these new G.I.'s marched off to war with cartons of Camel cigarettes in their knapsacks. There the similarity with the earlier conflict ended.

World War I was a European War. The doughboys, on the whole, had participated only in the final stages of a war in which the enemy was already on the road to defeat because of economic, rather than military, reasons. World War II was a total war, and its effects were felt directly at home. A few Japanese bombs fell on California. An American territory, Alaska, was invaded and occupied by troops under the flag of the Rising Sun. And the residents of Ocracoke, on the North Carolina Outer Banks, watched from shore the sinking of a British ship by a German submarine. Twin Citians vacationing in their cottages at Wrightsville and Carolina beaches in the summer of 1942 found, instead of the usual ghost crabs and sea oats, emplacements for the great coastal guns, which could fire on targets thirty miles at sea.

For the first time, American military units were not locally oriented. Boys from Winston-Salem found themselves training alongside boys from St. Paul, Minnesota, and Albuquerque, New Mexico. And when they got to what front there was, they found an enemy better prepared and equipped than they were. While Soviet troops, who bore the brunt of the early fighting in Europe, froze in Moscow and Leningrad, the men from Winston-Salem sweated in such unlikely spots as the deserts of North Africa and the tropical islands of the South Pacific.

Things were confusing at home, too. Local citizens read in the headlines of the daily papers such exotic names as Guadalcanal, Tunis, Iwo Jima, and Sicily. This total war was demanding. They had to give up luxuries that had come to be essentials. Tires, butter, gasoline, even clothes and cigarettes, the locally produced items, became scarce and the objects of rationing. A properly stamped piece of cardboard brought what money could not buy, unless one were willing to take his chances on the black market. But there was work for all who wanted it, and plenty of overtime, too, as the local plants, great and small, struggled to keep up with the demand for products.

There was plenty of money, but little time in which to spend it after long hours in the factories and the volunteer drives for War Bonds, scrap metal, and Red Cross packages for the troops. Local citizens, however, somehow found the time, in 1943, to put on the first Piedmont Festival of Music and Art. That same year the Food, Tobacco and Agricultural Workers—C.I.O., under the leadership of Robert Latham, Robert Black, Velma Hopkins, and Miranda Smith, organized Local 22 at the Reynolds Tobacco Company. On June 17, several thousand workers walked out, and, withstanding threats at home and from the War Labor Board, won a settlement of over one million dollars in retroactive pay. The first contract with the company was signed on April 24, 1944.

The city's new Smith Reynolds Airport attracted prompt attention. Within months of its opening the Directorate of Flying Safety of the Army Air Corps moved from Washington to Winston-Salem and built an operational complex at the airport. The improvements they made would help Smith Reynolds become one of the finest municipal air fields in the South in the post-war years.

As the tide began to turn in favor of the Allies, Winston-Salem men found themselves in the thick of the fighting. They rode the planes that bombed Hamburg and Dusseldorf and Dresden or island-hopped with the Navy and Marines from Saipan to Tarawa to Okinawa. When German Panzers led the last great counter-attack, local men fought in the bitter cold of the Ardennes Forest to foil the desperate gamble of a dying empire. By the time the top-hatted Japanese dignitaries put their names to the papers of surrender on board the *U.S.S. Missouri*, over two hundred Twin-Citians had died in battle, and another hundred were dead from other causes.

In 1941 the revamped Miller Municipal Airport was dedicated in memory of Zachary Smith Reynolds, who, with his older brother Dick, was a pioneer in local aviation. Taking to the air at age sixteen, he became, three years later, the youngest licensed transport pilot in the country. In 1931 he made the flight from England to China in an eighty horsepower amphibian. In that same year, at the age of twenty-one, he was killed at his father's Reynolda mansion under circumstances clouded by mystery to this day.

Courtesy of the Frank Jones Collection

The weary troops came home to the usual speeches and parades. But they had been sobered by what they saw in the theaters of combat. Two great enemies lay defeated, the Axis power and the depression. A return to normalcy in economic affairs meant that there was work to be done, and the citizens of Winston-Salem undertook it with relish. A revolution took place in local government, with the merger of the city and county Health Departments, the founding of the City-County Planning Board, and the establishment of a new City-Manager form of government.

Civic pride was a matter of course, and everybody wanted to get into the act. A campaign to bring in new industry, government services, and medical and educational facilities was successful. The Gray family gave the magnificent Graylyn estate to the Bowman Gray School of Medicine for future expansion and the Veterans' Administration established its state headquarters in the Twin City. The arts finally began to get their fair share of civic energy and funds with the founding of an Arts and Crafts Workshop and the Winston-Salem Symphony and Operetta associations. In the county centennial year, 1949, the Winston-Salem Arts Council, thought to be the second such operation in the nation, began its existence. The transportation industry began to catch up with demands for its services as the Hennis and Pilot motor freight lines joined the already established McLean, and Tom Davis expanded his Piedmont Aviation, founding, in 1948, Piedmont Airlines.

In the midst of all this positive activity, Local 22 struck Reynolds Tobacco Company. Adding its hysterical voice to that of the House Un-American Activities Committee, the *Winston-Salem Journal and Sentinel* began a campaign of scare tactics, with its primary focus on "red-baiting," against the union. As a result, the union lost its standing with the company. Earlier, union activists had played a major role in the voter registration drive that culminated with the election, in 1946, of the Reverend Kenneth Williams to the Board of Aldermen. He is thought to have been the first southern black to serve in such a capacity in the twentieth century. Now the black community rallied behind the strikers, and out of the ashes of apparent defeat came victory. Inadvertently, those who strove so relentlessly against the union had served as midwives at the birth of political and social awareness in the black community.

Winston-Salem found itself to be a true city, with all the problems that such a title implies. The citizens of the black and white communities determined to go stolidly forward, seeking to build at home a world resistant to the greater problems suffered in other places. It is fitting that one of the earliest manifestations of that attitude was the founding, in 1950, of Old Salem, Incorporated, dedicated to the preservation of the Moravian heritage of tranquility and good-will among all people.

The county centennial had been celebrated in 1949 with appropriate festivities, including the growing of beards by the more spirited men of the community. By the mid-1950s Winston-Salem had taken on the aspect of a modern city with the establishment of legal liquor stores, a television station, its first shopping center, a fabulous new park on the site of Will Reynolds' old farm, and, at last, the opening of the War Memorial Coliseum. Work on the Twin City's portion of the new system of national defense highways, the East-West expressway, had begun, and Ernie Shore Field, the most modern minor league baseball park in the nation, replaced the antiquated, but fondly remembered, Southside Ball Park.

In 1958, the city's biggest industry made the first of what would be many diversification moves with the founding of Archer Aluminum. And that year the death knell of the downtown district was struck with the opening, in a wealthy western suburb, of the James G. Hanes Community Center, which would eventually house such organizations as the Chamber of Commerce, the Winston-Salem Symphony, and the Arts Council. Faced with the desertion of these civic organizations, the deterioration of the city center was only a matter of time.

In 1959 Winston-Salem received the first of two All-American City awards. A second would be conferred in 1964, by which time urban renewal would have become a fact of life in the Twin City. The urban renewal program was instituted to eliminate slums, the existence of which had been denied by the mayor in a communication with Federal authorities in the early thirties, and to revitalize the central business district. Whole city blocks were leveled and imposing new structures erected. In 1966 the Moravian village, now known as Old Salem, celebrated its bicentennial.

In 1943 Malcom McLean moved his fledgling trucking business from Red Spring to this site on Waughtown Street. The company rapidly grew into one of the largest in the world and helped to make Winston-Salem a motor freight center. Behind the McLean building can be seen two of the city's oldest wood-working firms, the Phillips Lumber Company, and beyond it, the Fogle Furniture Company, founded in 1923.

Courtesy of the McLean Trucking Company

The massive surge in manufacture of war materials quickly depleted available supplies of all metals in the United States. Scrap metal drives rivaled War Bond campaigns as matters of importance. Here, volunteers empty the collection pen on the square beneath the Confederate monument.

Courtesy of the Frank Jones Collection

By then many of Winston-Salem's young men found themselves again at war, this time against the most baffling enemy of all. While they battled the phantom Viet Cong guerillas in the delta of the Mekong River, the country was torn apart by clashes between the masters of war and a steadily increasing throng of anti-war protestors. After eight bloody and fruitless years, the United States withdrew, leaving Viet Nam and most of the rest of Southeast Asia in ruins. Army Medical Specialist Lawrence Joel, a black man from Winston-Salem, was awarded the Congressional Medal of Honor for his heroism during a Viet Cong attack.

Ringed by shopping centers and malls, the heart of Winston-Salem was fast falling into disrepair. Emergency first aid, in the form of a downtown mall, was applied, but failed. The arrival of the Joseph Schlitz Brewing Company's new plant, the largest single brewing building in the world, brought a substantial economic boost, but did little for the downtown area. A further blow to the city center was the decision of R. J. Reynolds to locate its new world headquarters in the suburbs. But the urban business leaders would not all give up.

By the beginning of the nation's bicentennial year, the downtown area had a flashy new Hyatt House Hotel across from the Benton Convention Center on Fifth Street, and a complex housing the North Carolina National Bank and Winston-Salem Savings and Loan along Liberty and Third Streets. Early in that year the new Hall of Justice, between Main and Liberty Streets, opened, replacing Forsyth County's third courthouse, to be followed by the completion of the new Federal Building, across the street, on Main. As retail establishments continued to move into the shopping centers and malls, a new effort was announced in the late spring of 1976 to solve the problems plaguing the old business district.

Two projects with potential as aids in the revitalization effort were announced. The North Carolina School of the Arts began negotiations for the restoration of the magnificent old Carolina Theater building as a performance center for their productions, and Historic Winston, Incorporated, opened the Winston-Salem Museum in the former Wachovia Bank Building, the city's oldest skyscraper.

By early 1977 the establishment of the North Carolina Historical Preservation Fund added another ray of hope for the disorganized handful of citizens who truly cared about Winston's heritage. With so much energy and funding being poured into Old Salem, indifference to Winston's plight would be their greatest enemy in their battle against the redevelopment mentality that gripped those in control.

Winston's skyline as it appeared after the second
World War is a blend of the old and the new. At left
is the spire of the First Baptist Church (1925), an
evocation of the European tradition, then the Robert
E. Lee Hotel (1921), the Reynolds Building (1928), the
Nissen Building (1927), and the Carolina Hotel (1928).
Between the Reynolds and Nissen buildings are the
O'Hanlon Building (1915), the Pepper Building (1928),
and the old Wachovia Bank Building (1911). The
white cupola near the center marks the Journal and
Sentinel Building (1927). Standing up for the old in
the center foreground are three houses built between
1880 and 1910 by, from left to right, H. D.
Poindexter, T. L. Vaughn, and J. J. Brooks.

Photo by Frank Jones

Looking east from the Nissen Building around 1946,
we find the city to be much the same as it was at the
beginning of the Great Depression. Just beyond the
Reynolds Building on Linden Street are the Brown
Brothers' tobacco warehouse (1895), four-and-one-half
stories with a mansard roof and dormer windows, and
the tobacco factory of W. F. Smith and Sons (1890),
with a gable roof and stepped-gable facade, now a part
of the Piedmont Leaf Tobacco Company complex.
Near the center, at Patterson and Third, rises the
crenelated tower of the S. J. Nissen Wagon Works
(circa 1900), a major blacksmith operation which
produced very few wagons. Beyond the factory district
is part of East Winston's residential area, essentially
demolished by urban redevelopment in the 1960s.

Courtesy of Historic Winston

The intersection of Fourth and Broad Streets, at upper left, provides the key for this 1946 photograph. From left to right on the south side of Fourth are the Greek Orthodox Church (1909) and the house built by G. A. Follin (circa 1890), now demolished. Across Broad is the brand new Modern Chevrolet building, followed by, on the west side of Green Street, the structure housing Hutchins' Drug Store and the Winston-Salem Broadcasting Company, WTOB. On the north side of Fourth, at the corner of Broad Street, stands the First Christian Church. The next block, later occupied by the Sears-Roebuck Department Store, is the site of the West End School (1884). At lower left is the Gray Court Apartments (1929), the Twin City's first large complex. In the foreground on Fifth Street are the homes of L. A. Vaughn (circa 1895), F. M. Bohannon (circa 1895), and a portion of the Sandel Rosenbacher house (1908-09).

Courtesy of Historic Winston

In 1940 twenty year old Tom Davis began Piedmont Aviation, incorporating a charter air service with aircraft instruction, sales, and maintenance. Five years later, at the end of World War II, he had a staff of thirty-five and a yen for expansion. In 1948, his Piedmont Airlines began service on its first route between Wilmington and Cincinnati. The company is now an important regional feeder, serving the central Appalachian corridor.

Courtesy of Historic Winston

The National Association of Stock Car Racing had its beginnings on primitive dirt tracks in dozens of southern towns. Alvin Hawkins and others in Winston-Salem were among the founders, running their races on such as the Peace Haven Speedway, above, off Peace Haven Road, in the late forties and early fifties. Soon a regular Saturday night program was established at Bowman Gray Stadium, where the smells of Castrol and scorched rubber and the occasional infield fistfights would draw capacity crowds. There were local heroes: "Perk" Brown, "Shorty" York, and the Myers brothers, Bobby and Billy. But the Bowman Gray track served as a proving ground for some of NASCARS's biggest names: Lee Petty, father of NASCARS's all-time winner Richard Petty; Curtis Turner; Glenn Wood; Jim Paschal; and "Buck" Baker, father of current front runner "Buddy" Baker, and a man who, thought to be washed up, would win the "Southern 500" at Darlington, South Carolina, in 1964.

Courtesy of the Frank Jones Collection

The Dixie Classic Fair is North Carolina's finest, and had its beginnings at the old fairgrounds on Liberty Street. Here the "World of Mirth" midway beckons fairgoers, around 1950, with the usual sideshows, games of chance, and three giant Ferris wheels.

Courtesy of Historic Winston

197

On October 16, 1951, President Harry S. Truman
broke the ground for the first construction on the new
Wake Forest College site. Dr. Harold Tribble, right,
Wake Forest president, seemed pleased.

Courtesy of the Frank Jones Collection

By the early 1950s, commercial development had begun to make serious inroads in Winston's former "Millionaire's Row" along Spruce and Fifth Streets. On Spruce, the Victorian delights of W. P. Hill, J. K. Norfleet, and Dr. John Bynum had made way for the expanding newspaper and insurance empires, while on Fifth, the First Baptist Church had replaced Robah Gray's house. Gone also were the mansions of F. L. Gorrell and R. J. Reynolds. Mr. Gorrell's house, at the corner of Poplar and Fifth, was replaced by a flat, ugly building emphasized by the swooping rotunda and graceful tower of the First Baptist Church across the street. And, as if to compensate for the characterless hulk facing it, the Centenary Methodist Church, designed by Goodhue Associates, New York, and completed in 1931, at a cost in excess of one and-one-quarter million dollars, lent its Gothic charm to the changing face of Winston's second major residential neighborhood.

Photo by Frank Jones

Frank Jones stood near Spring Street to get this twilight view of West Fourth Street. At left is Marion D. West's Winston Motor Mart, next door to the residence of George L. Adams, later torn down for a parking lot. The Winston was the Twin City's newest theatre, with air conditioning, but without the elegance of the old Carolina. Beyond the theatre were the Winstonette Restaurant, and, behind it, the Twentieth Century Bowling Alley, featuring duckpins. Next door stood the Dutch Treat Sandwich Shop. Across the street, from the right, are the Alexander Apartments, and, out of sight behind them, the residence of Samuel B. Baird, next to Doby's Bakery. Farther up in the row of shops and small businesses was the Chicken-in-the-Basket Restaurant. At the time of this 1952 photograph the Winston was one of eight downtown theatres. Today there are two, and the Winston is the older.

Courtesy of Historic Winston

The citizens of America's small cities had always exuded a smug aloofness when the topic of international politics was broached. But the "cold war" era of the forties and fifties changed all that. In Winston-Salem the Western Electric Company manufactured the guidance system for the new "Nike" ballistic missiles. Maps were passed around that identified the Twin City as a primary, or at least, secondary, target, in the Soviet "first-strike plan." Besides, everybody knows that you can't fight a war without cigarettes, and R. J. Reynolds just happened to be the number one producer in the world. Here, the pigeons on Trade Street are not witness to the premature death of the central business district. They just could not find an air raid shelter. If the sirens screamed on a school day, delighted children were taught to crawl under their desks. They, and those who devised such a ploy, had not yet seen the films of Hiroshima and Nagasaki.

Courtesy of the Frank Jones Collection

The Union Bus Depot (1941) and the Robert E. Lee Hotel (1921) no longer grace Cherry Street between Fourth and Fifth as they did in this mid-fifties view, but Norman-Stockton is a determined advocate of the movement to preserve the central business district of the Twin City.

Courtesy of Historic Winston

In 1953, the independent spirit that had inhibited Taylor Brothers for seventy years finally gave up the ghost. The company was absorbed by the American Snuff Company, although continuing operation under the old name. Here a part of the nineteenth century factory complex, located at First and Patterson Streets, is seen at the time of sale. At the right was the old W. B. Ellis Tobacco Factory, later acquired by the Taylors. In the fall of 1976 the entire complex was intact, with the Ellis plant, one of the oldest still standing in the city, virtually unchanged externally from its 1890s appearance. Within a few months the Ellis plant had been demolished, becoming another victim of the shortsighted redevelopment movement.

Courtesy of Bill East

Chestnut Street between Second and Third was an early center of the restaurant and lunch-room business, catering to the tobacco trade. Here, in the early 1950s, the block opposite R. J. Reynolds' number 256 complex boasts eleven cafes, in addition to two garages, a dry cleaning establishment, and one vacant building. The smell of beans, hot dogs, and french fries has been replaced by the odor of exhaust fumes and hot brake linings.

Courtesy of the Frank Jones Collection

The 1954 Supreme Court decision in *Brown vs. Board of Education*, announced while French paratroopers were making their last ditch effort at Dien Bien Phu, had no effect in Winston-Salem for three years. In the summer of 1957, however, racist rabble-rouser John Kasper arrived in town to protest the planned integration of Reynolds High School that coming fall. Kasper held forth beneath the Confederate monument on the square, but his attempts to fan the flames of racial hatred failed. On September 5, Gwendolyn Yvonne Bailey (left, above) accompanied by a newswoman and a magazine correspondent, became the first black to enter a white school in Winston-Salem. She was fifteen years old. The small crowd of curiosity seekers gathered off-campus never even caught sight of her. The night before, die-hards had painted racist slogans on the school's circular drive, but early-arriving students walked across the ugly epithets without a glance. Soon, service club members had obliterated the scrawlings while the cameras of *Life, Look,* and other national publications clicked away. Later, while National Guardsmen prowled the halls of Little Rock's Central High, Gwen Bailey went peacefully about her business in the Twin City. There were incidents, all of them minor and mostly personal. The bulk of R. J. R.'s students were more interested in the football team that would go on to be state co-champions.

Photo by Frank Jones

An omen of things to come, Thruway Shopping Center, Winston-Salem's first, nestles in the curve of the right-of-way of Interstate 40 in the late fifties. WTOB-TV held teen-age dance parties, featuring the music of Fats Domino, Buddy Holly, the Diamonds, and the Coasters, in the parking lot beneath their tower at upper left. The A & P store at lower right would later become a bowling alley, and the Triangle Drive-In restaurant would be built just below it, providing a new cruising spot for teenagers on the prowl.

Courtesy of Historic Winston

During the presidential administrations of John F. Kennedy and Lyndon B. Johnson, the Civil Rights Movement in the South made great strides toward attaining basic human rights for blacks. The result was a resurgence in the activities of the Ku Klux Klan, one of whose speakers is silhouetted by the traditional burning cross at a meeting in Piedmont North Carolina. In Alabama, Georgia, and Mississippi, Klansmen perpetrated a number of murders, fire-bombings, and other assorted atrocities. Nearby Guilford County was a hotbed of Klan activity, but the determination of local leaders kept Winston-Salem and Forsyth County relatively free of overt Kluxer influence.

Courtesy of the Frank Jones Collection

Still, the Twin City was not the integrated paradise it seemed. In early November 1967, rioting broke out along North Liberty Street in the commercial districts bordered by extensive black neighborhoods. The trigger was the killing of a black man by policemen who were attempting to arrest him. Arson, looting, and indiscriminate shooting were the order of the day. National Guard troops were called in, and for the first time since 1918, armored vehicles on official business were seen on the city streets. In the midst of strict curfews and an area-wide ban on the sale of alcoholic beverages, Frank Jones took this picture that summed up the futility and frustrations felt by many of the black rioters.

Photo by Frank Jones

At 7:30 a.m., Sunday, March 26, 1972, three hundred charges of dynamite, set in the basement and first floor of the Robert E. Lee Hotel, exploded, and in less than ten seconds a city landmark for half a century was merely a two-story pile of rubble. It was a crisp, sunny morning, enhanced by a blanket of snow from one of winter's last gasps. But when the show was over, the snow in the downtown area was covered by a layer of dust as much as a quarter of an inch thick. City crews spent the rest of the day hosing down buildings and streets in an attempt to get rid of the dust. Those travelers who slept there and local people who attended dances on the Balinese roof will never forget the Robert E. Lee. The site is now occupied by the Hyatt House.

Courtesy of the Frank Jones Collection

A mad admixture of parking lots and decks and squared-off boxes for offices squeeze in upon Winston-Salem's first "skyscraper," the old Wachovia Bank Building at center, and most adventurous project, the Reynolds Building. Many Twin Citians are taking the sign at the left literally and doing their shopping elsewhere.

Photo by Fam Brownlee

The story of a city is told in one magnificent photograph, the twin monuments of commerce and industry rising between the artifacts of their beginnings.

Photo by Frank Jones

Acknowledgements

In any undertaking of this scope, the assistance of many people is required if success is to be achieved. I must express my deepest appreciation to Bill East, for selflessly offering his substantial collection of photographs and his considerable knowledge of local history, and to Doctor Frank P. Albright, whose help in gaining access to the Frank Jones picture collection was invaluable. Ann Correll and the staff of the North Carolina Room of the Forsyth County Public Library provided not only courteous service, but many tips and leads to things that I would otherwise have missed. Frances Griffin and other staff members at Old Salem, Incorporated helped in getting some otherwise unobtainable pictures and patiently answered the many questions needed to identify them. A special appreciation is due to Terrell Young, Joe Bradshaw, and Blanche Morgan Hobson, whose personal interest in and stories about the early history of Winston helped uncover many little-known events, and to the many individuals who spent time looking for and loaned or gave me their family pictures.

Nothing has been included in this book for which corroboration could not be obtained. Errors, however, are an all too human certainty. For any and all that occur, I alone am responsible.

The scene of the first foothold of the Unitas Fratrum in Piedmont North Carolina is now a park, administered by the City Recreation Department. The restored church of 1788 coexists peacefully with the reconstructed stockade of the French and Indian War. Excavated foundations reveal the sites of most of Behabara's early buildings, set below the hilltop God's Acre. Despite the increasing flow of traffic on Bethabara Road, it is a place of quietude, serving as a fit monument to those hardy settlers of the House of Passage.

Photo by Fam Brownlee